WRETCHED WRITING

WRETCHED WRITING

WRITING

A Compendium of Crimes
Against the English Language

ROSS PETRAS AND KATHRYN PETRAS

A PERIGEE BOOK

A PERIGEE BOOK
Published by the Penguin Group
Penguin Group (USA) Inc.
375 Hudson Street, New York, New York 10014, USA

USA I Canada I UK I Ireland I Australia I New Zealand I India I South Africa I China

Penguin Books Ltd., Registered Offices: 80 Strand, London WC2R 0RL, England
For more information about the Penguin Group, visit penguin.com.

Library of Congress Cataloging-in-Publication Data

Petras, Kathryn.
Wretched writing : a compendium of crimes against the English language / Kathryn Petras and
Ross Petras. — First edition.
pages cm
Includes index.
ISBN 978-0-399-15924-4 (pbk.)
1. Authorship—Humor.   2. English language—Style—Humor.
3. English language—Terms and phrases—Humor.   4. Style, Literary—Humor.
5. Clichés.   I. Petras, Ross.   II. Title.
PN6231.A77P48   2013
808.02'0207—dc23   2013009307

First edition: August 2013

PRINTED IN THE UNITED STATES OF AMERICA

10 9 8 7 6 5 4 3 2 1

Text design by Laura K. Corless

While the authors have made every effort to provide accurate telephone numbers, Internet addresses,
and other contact information at the time of publication, neither the publisher nor the authors assume
any responsibility for errors, or for changes that occur after publication. Further, the publisher does
not have any control over and does not assume any responsibility for author or third-party websites or
their content.

Most Perigee books are available at special quantity discounts for bulk purchases for sales promotions,
premiums, fund-raising, or educational use. Special books, or book excerpts, can also be created to fit
specific needs. For details, write: Special.Markets@us.penguingroup.com.

ACKNOWLEDGMENTS

We must give resounding praise and heartfelt thanks to the other connoisseurs and collectors of wretched writing, both those who came before us and those who are still active in the field. So let us doff our caps to the intrepid pioneers D. B. Wyndham-Lewis and Charles Lee (*The Stuffed Owl*) as well as puerile poetry pundit Nicholas T. Parsons (*The Joy of Bad Verse*); the estimable Nick Page (*In Search of the World's Worst Writers*), the prolifically profound Bill Pronzini (*Gun in Cheek, Son of Gun in Cheek,* and *Six Gun in Cheek*), Peter Haining and his wry *Wrotten English,* Richard Polt and his excellent Keeler Society, Janice Harayda and her witty Delete Key awards, the truly mighty Thog and his Masterclass in the SF newsletter *Ansible,* Don Watson and his wonderful website *Weasel Words,* the *Literary Review* and their annual Bad Sex in Fiction awards, Adam Cadre and his big-in-our-eyes Lyttle Lytton Contest—Found division (not to be confused with the *big* Bulwer-Lytton contest, which features only made-up bad writing), Peter Harrington and his erudite *Cataloguer's Desk* blog, as well as the many eagle-eyed people who, through the years, have sent us examples of wretched writing for our calendar, *The 365 Stupidest Things Ever Said* (well, written in this case . . .). We couldn't have done this book without them.

And, of course, we couldn't have done it without our amazingly able agent, Andrea Somberg; our fabulously fantastic families, Sly, Alex, and Mom; and our exceptionally erudite editor, Meg Leder. And here let us stop, as we're getting alarmingly alliterative . . . (Such are the dangers of immersing ourselves in wretched writing!)

INTRODUCTION

There is much written about writing . . . or rather "good" writing. There are numerous books on how to write novels that sell, how to craft riveting dialogue, how to make an academic paper actually say something coherent, how to make advertising copy sizzle, how to develop realistic characters—in short, how to write well.

This book is not one of those books.

It is not about the kind of writing people in their right mind would want to write or read. It's about the *other* kind of writing, the kind of writing that makes one want to hurl an offending book (or one's lunch) across the room. This is the writing we've termed "wretched."

Wretched writing is, to put it politely, a felonious assault on the English language. It is the lowest of the low. It plumbs the depths of literature and spelunks in the caves of nonfiction.

In other words, it stinks.

But what specifically makes writing wretched? Like its kissing cousin, pornography, wretched writing is difficult to precisely define. To paraphrase a Supreme Court justice, one knows it when one sees it. And just like pornography, wretched writing comes in numerous and quite varied forms and modes—although, sadly, it is not as profitable. It can be rendered (or should we say "performed"?) by a good writer on a bad day, or more often, all the time by a dyed-in-the-wool wretched writer who can do no better. One finds wretched writing almost anywhere: in passages exhibiting a blatant ignorance of the constraints of grammar and in exuberantly and brazenly excessive prose. Wretched writing can be marked by overusage of literary tropes or underusage of good taste.

Wretched writing also knows no era. We can assume that it stretches back to the beginning of the written word, when some Sumerian scribe incised the wrong signs for oxen on a clay tablet. Sometimes writing is wretched in retrospect, as when we look back and laugh at some overly ornate piece of Victorian-era poetry or prose. But most wretched writing is timeless. It *was* wretched, it *is* wretched, and it *shall be* wretched forever.

In short, wretched writing is simply very bad writing. Very bad writing in all the glittering array of fascinating possibilities. And therein lies one of its fascinations: Rest assured—if there is a way of saying something well, there is also a way of saying the same thing badly. Horribly, terribly, clunkily, and very amusingly badly. With atrociously bad grammar, clanking syntax, wooden dialogue of oaken hardness, terrible transitions, dull imagery, clichéd clichés. Wretched writers are intrepid; they boldly go where no writer has gone before and create creative and innovatively new categories of terribly awful prose and poetry.

Thus this book, an alphabetically organized celebration of the most wretched writing imaginable. In reading *Wretched Writing*, you will go on a tour of that which is the worst, the most awful, and of course, the funniest in crimes committed against the English language—from A (adjectives, excessive use of) to Z (zoological sexual encounters, politician-writers and). Along the way, you'll stop at such diverse topics as "body parts and bodily fluids, peripatetic," "celebrity faux-thors," "food imagery, bad," "non sequiturs," "redundancy, repetitive," and of course, "hysterical historical dialogue."

You'll meet the wretchedest of the wretched writers themselves, people like detective novelist Harry Stephen Keeler, who foisted characters such as "Flying Strangler-Baby" on an unsuspecting public, and sci-fi novelist Lionel Fanthorpe, who, during one three-year period, wrote a new novel every twelve days. (Reading his prose, one can see that this is not as impressive as it sounds . . .) You'll find entries from repeat offenders, such as the above-mentioned Keeler and Fanthorpe, as well as Amanda McKittrick Ros and James Corbett—the acknowledged superstars in the field of bad writing. In these cases, their wretched writing is so unequivocally wretched, we feel we are in the presence of genius . . . of a sort.

You'll meet some very *good* writers as well, including such literary luminaries as Norman Mailer, D. H. Lawrence, and Martin Amis. Yes, we *all* have our wretched writing moments, even the very best of us.

And as you savor these deliciously dreadful samples, you'll learn how *not* to write.

We also hope you'll laugh a lot.

adjectives, excessive use of: Some writers seem to think that nouns are like infants—they should not be left unaccompanied. Never. So every time a noun appears in their work, it has an adjective modifying it. Someone doesn't just have teeth, he has "white teeth" that show in a "feral smile," or "cheerful smile," or "sad smile."

Of course, a well-chosen adjective helps the reader visualize the scene, but these adjective addicts take it a step too far. In their hands, not one noun is left uncompromised. The result can be a bit . . . exhausting.

> Her slim arms, agile as darting javelins, alternately waved and reined, fluttering the open collared, gray, pearl-buttoned waist that she wore with her chamois-colored riding costume and striking tan boots and copper-hued chaps encasing her mobile thighs with whipping jacket tails.
>
> —Samuel Alexander White,
> *Called Northwest* (1943)

[Ed. note: We were hoping at least her thighs could have remained plain old thighs . . .]

> In the center, a little toward the back wall, stood a raised stone altar, in the form of a large simply hewn crude stone with a somewhat concave surface, round like a very shallow wide bowl.
>
> —Vera Nazarian, *Lords of Rainbow* (2004)

[Ed. note: In fairness, "center" is not adjectived. It must have been an oversight.]

For sheer exhaustive overachievement in adjective addiction, we submit the following passages culled from one book:

> A blindingly handsome young man was sitting on one of the barstools nursing an imported beer. His dark, straight hair was pulled back into a tight tail that fell over his shoulder and brushed his forearm. His pale, chiseled face was pared to the bone showing fine, sharp features and full lips that belonged on the cover of a pulp vampire novel . . .
>
> Jennifer, her tastefully made-up face wreathed with a deep scarlet smile, came thumping up the tiny staircase in her shiny, black plastic, platform boots. She practically danced with excitement into the circular boots . . .
>
> Jennifer giggled, struggling to sit in her exquisitely short, super tight, red plastic skirt. Daintily, she crossed her legs, exposing a long line of trim, black fishnet-encased thigh . . .
>
> Jennifer licked her artfully painted lips and darted a look over her shoulder, tossing her short and stylish, bright blond bob that curled around her ears.
>
> —Morgan Hawke, *House of Shadows* (2004)

But Hawke is still a piker compared to the legend that is Pel Torro (aka Lionel Fanthorpe):

The things were odd, weird, grotesque. There was something horribly uncustomary and unwonted about them. They were completely unfamiliar. Their appearance was outlandish and extraordinary. Here was something quite phenomenal about them. They were supernormal; they were unparalleled; they were unexampled. The shape of the aliens was singular in every sense. They were curious, odd, queer, peculiar and fantastic, and yet when every adjective had been used on them, when every preternatural epithet had been applied to their aberrant and freakish appearance, when everything that could be said about such eccentric, exceptional, anomalous creatures had been said, they still remained indescribable in any concrete terms.

—Pel Torro (Lionel Fanthorpe),
Galaxy 666 (1968)

Indescribable indeed.

◇◇◇◇◇

adjectives, wrong: Overuse of adjectives is not the only way wretched writers abuse the ostensibly inoffensive describing words. There are also numerous cases wherein said writers might not use too many adjectives but simply the *wrong* adjectives. Thus the reader is faced with somewhat perplexing images that seem to have come from a bizarro world in which watches can have confused sexual identities, furniture is dead, and a deep suntan makes one resemble a . . . plant?

> She popped the elastic at the top of the second sock and pushed her sexually ambiguous Timex watch up along the blond hairs of her handsome forearms.
>
> —Steve Whalen, *POB2, A Love Story* (1982)

> And stark naked, he went out into the hall, striding, a strange, white figure between the unliving furniture. He came back with the towels . . .
>
> —D. H. Lawrence, *Women in Love* (1920)

> It came to Stafford that the man would be a Hindu, of one of the southern Indian states where the races are sunbaked to a dark green.
>
> —H. L. Gates, *Death Counts Five* (1934)

◇◇◇◇◇

alliteration, obsessive: Alliteration—repeating the same initial sound in a series of words (like Peter Piper picked, etc., etc.)—can be good. But it also can be bad. The wretched writer sometimes wields this literary device like a bulky burdensome bludgeon, battering the innocent reader into a pulsating pulullating pulp. Ahem. Excuse us for that.

The heroine of bad alliteration is Victorian novelist Amanda McKittrick Ros, whose exuberant use of alliterative titles—*Irene Iddesleigh* (novel), *Delina Delaney* (novel), *Poems of Puncture* (poetry), *Fumes of Formation* (poetry), *Helen Huddleston* (posthumous novel)—provides ominous warning of the alliterative horrors lurking between the covers. But let us, to use a Rosian phrase, "firm our flanks" and take a somewhat random peek at what awaits:

> The living sometimes learn the touchy tricks of the traitor, the tardy and the tempted; the dead have evaded the flighty earthy future, and form to swell the retinue of retired rights, the righteous school of the invisible and the rebellious roar of the raging nothing.
>
> —*Irene Iddesleigh* (1897)

◇

> Madame Pear had a swell staff of sweet-faced helpers swathed in stratagem, whose members and garments glowed with the lust of the loose, sparkled with the tears of the tortured, shone with the sunlight of bribery, dangled with the diamonds of distrust, slashed with sapphires of scandals.
>
> —*Helen Huddleson* (posthumous, 1969)

In closing, may we simply add: Always avoid excessive, exaggerated, exorbitant, execrable alliteration.

analogies, bad and excessively extended: An analogy is a literary device by which one (the writer) likens two dissimilar objects, pointing out the sometimes unexpected or hidden features they have in common. A simile ("His brain was like a concrete block") is what's called an expressed analogy; while a metaphor ("His brain was a concrete block") is an implied one (see page 128). We, of course, know that his brain can't *literally* be a concrete block; that's why this is a literary device. But we assume you know this. Unless your brain is a concrete block. (If it's *like* a concrete block, see similes, bad, page 177.)

For our purposes—since we discuss both similes and metaphors elsewhere, here we examine the wretchedly *extended* use of analogy, the cases where an overenthusiastic writer immerses himself gleefully and wholeheartedly in the soupy stew of what he or she *thinks* is a clever comparison between two dissimilar objects. A few examples:

Person-as-Planet Analogy

Her hand is moving away from my knee and heading north. Heading unnervingly and with a steely will towards the pole. And, like Sir Ranulph Fiennes, Pamela will not easily be discouraged. I try twitching, and then shaking my leg, but to no avail. At last, disastrously, I try squeezing her hand painfully between my bony thighs, but this only serves to inflame her ardour the more. Ever northward moves her hand, while she smiles languorously at my right ear. And when she reaches the north pole, I think in wonder and terror . . . She will surely want to pitch her tent.

—Christopher Hart,
Rescue Me (2001)

Person-as-Continent Analogy

[T]he most tousled, tangled pubic patch through which I have ever had to find my way. A near impenetrable little forest, a small private Amazon to get lost in. But when one finally got down to the river, slipping and sliding through reeds and weeds and rushes and undergrowth, one could slither through the mud and dive in, wholly immerse oneself, stay down for an impossibly long time, nearly drowning, before coming up again, panting and heaving . . .

—André Brink, *Before I Forget* (2004)

[Ed. note: Aside from the irritating analogy, we must also note that clearly this character is in dire need of some depilatory work.]

Person's-Mental-State-as-Deep-Sea-Diver Analogy (With Special Bonus Added Chair and Octopus Analogies)

> Her spirits suddenly started to ascend with the speed of a diver who has suddenly kicked off his lead shoes—except that, unfortunately for poor Elsa, the long slimy clammy tentacle of a huge octopus at that moment reached up from the sea bottom and took tight hold of Mr. Diver, the tentacle consisting of the ineluctable fact that by this very letter Saul Moffitt must—would—sit in the chair on whose handle, anyway, Richard St. George was now sitting.
>
> —Harry Stephen Keeler,
> *The Man with the Wooden Spectacles* (1941)

[Ed. note: While we are gripped by the extended concept of deep-sea diving, particularly "octopus tentacle as letter," we are also a tad confused—where did the chair come from? Is it the diver's chair? In other words, what?]

Marketing-as-Mixed Drinks

Let's take the cosmopolitan: four parts vodka, two parts cranberry juice, two parts triple sec, one part lime juice, a lime rind, and a swizzle stick. These symbolize your marketing mix—with vodka as the basic, proven sales ingredient (say direct mail, Internet marketing), cranberry juice as your long-term branding and advertising efforts, triple sec as promotions, lime juice as PR, and the lime rind and swizzle stick as experimental efforts (like mobile marketing). What should you do to keep serving martinis in a way that lets you make money today while keeping your clientele coming back for more?

—Mike Linton,
"Why Marketing Is Like Making Martinis,"
Forbes.com (April 28, 2009)

◇◇◇◇◇

anatomy, problematic: Anatomy is a rather basic background element in writing. While a writer usually doesn't overtly address subjects anatomical, he or she incorporates its simple rules in his or her work. In other words, legs walk, arms wave, and feet flex, and other body parts behave in anatomically correct ways.

That said, for some reason it is not uncommon to find the human body behaving rather peculiarly in certain wretchedly written works. In these cases, it appears that the writers have tossed away the rules of basic anatomy, allowing their characters a certain . . . flexibility, let us say. And flexibility is indeed an apt word, as sometimes characters perform amazing gymnastic feats better suited to contortionists:

> She sat huddled in a chair, covering her ears with crossed legs.
>
> —Edgar Jepson,
> "The Moment of Truth" (posthumous, 1949)

And in another example of (apparently) extreme "bendiness" (or simply missing legs and torso):

> He lifted her tee-shirt over her head. Her silk panties followed.
>
> —Peter F. Hamilton, *Mindstar Rising* (1993)

Sometimes the anatomical problem isn't excessive flexibility, but a body part doing something that one usually doesn't read about—chiefly because it is impossible:

> Then Marshall squeezed his eyes shut and nodded his torso a few times . . .
>
> —Ramsey Campbell, *The One Safe Place* (1996)

◇

> She stood at the foot of the stairs, narrowing her eyes and breathing through her hips.
>
> —From a short story in *The Saturday Evening Post*

◇

> Talbert's toes whipped like pennants in a gale.
>
> —Richard Matheson, "The Splendid Source" (1956)

◇

> He encircled her hand with his arm . . .
>
> —Marion Zimmer Bradley, *Endless Voyage* (1975)

People who leaned over backwards, McCullough
thought grimly, frequently fell flat on their face . . .

       —James White, *All Judgment Fled* (1968)

◇◇◇◇◇

anticlimaxes, unfortunate: Missing out on climaxes in the
literary act of reading is as bad as missing out on climaxes in the
physical act of love. At least in our opinions. This is why many
wretched writers leave us unfulfilled.

Instead of building up intensity, and arranging words, clauses,
and sentences in their order of importance until the story or idea
reaches an exhilarating peak, the wretched writer loses steam, as
it were. He builds us up and then lets us down, teases us into
missing our literary orgasm. He ends with an anticlimax instead
of its opposite.

Here are three classic and mercifully short anticlimaxes.

First it made him furiously angry, then apoplectic, then
diabolically insane with rage, and for the last quarter
of an hour it affected his stomach.

       —James Corbett, *Red Dagger* (1934)

◇

I could hardly wait to begin the investigation.
Somehow, I firmly believed that (at last!) we were

following a course that would clearly reveal—
something!

—W. Shepard Pleasants,
The Stingaree Murders (1932)

◇

The Kid came out of the rain and walked in on Death.
It was as unexpected as having your hat slide down
over your ears.

—Abel Shott, *The Bullet Brand* (1947)

Now for the longer, more annoying type of anticlimax, in which we invest time and effort into reading only to end up with a dull thud—in this case in the person of a B-grade Mexican movie character.

And he came hard in her mouth and his dick jumped around and rattled on her teeth and he blacked out and she took his dick out of her mouth and lifted herself from his face and whipped the pillow away and he gasped and glugged at the air, and he came again so hard that his dick wrenched out of her hand and a shot of it hit him straight in the eye and stung like nothing he'd ever had in there, and he yelled with the pain, but the yell could have been anything, and as she grabbed at his dick, which was leaping around like a shower dropped in an empty bath, she scratched his back deeply with the nails of both hands and he shot three more times, in thick stripes on her chest. Like Zorro.

—Giles Coren, *Winkler* (2005)

[Ed. note: This passage is not as graphic as you maybe think. "Dick" here refers to a gun, not the dangly male apparatus that shoots things other than bullets.]

Some novels are arranged such that the entire plot ends with an annoying anticlimax, but we won't subject you to that here. Instead, let's look at a newspaper story which takes an anticlimactic turn that only a passionate mycologist would fail to recognize . . .

WINCHESTER (AP)—A scientist told 182 Shenandoah University graduates to avoid complacency.

"Hitch your wagon to a star. Keep your seat and there you are," Charlotte C. Campbell said. "I can only hope your star is as exciting and rewarding to you as mine was to me."

Ms. Campbell has studied fungi for more than 40 years.

—*The Richmond Times-Dispatch* (May 18, 1991)

There is also the anticlimactic obituary, here ending in unexciting nonferrous metallurgy and foodstuffs.

Pyongyang, December 20 (KCNA)—The people in South Hamgyong Province are now stricken with deep grief, upon hearing the sad news that leader Kim Jong

Il passed away of a sudden illness on his way to field guidance. They are now mourning his demise with bitter grief, picturing to themselves the image of kind-hearted Kim Jong Il who visited various places of the province shortly ago to indicate an orientation and ways for putting on a fresh higher phase the overall economic work including the production of vinalon and fertilizers, geothermal equipment, varieties of custom-built facilities, mineral and nonferrous metals, fruit and grain.

—From the official North Korean website

And penultimately (see also words, wrong, on page 198) we read with rising interest of the perils of the frozen wastes of Antarctica, only to end with food containers.

All the men were acutely aware of the tremendous events taking place: the change in the earth's axis; the great earthquakes which had apparently occurred; the sudden eruptions of many old and new volcanoes; the breaking up of the Great Ross Ice Shelf; the torrents of meltwater, and evident speeding up of the flood of glacial ice tossing thousands of giant icebergs into the sea. Making several trips, they brought out many cans. Some of them were dented.

—Edwin Woodard and Heather Woodard Bischoff,
Storehouses of the Snow (1980)

Lastly, to sum up our opinion of the anticlimax:

It beats the devil. It's diabolical. It's fiendish. It's just
not right.

—Florence Mae Pettee,
The Palgrave Mummy (1929)

◇◇◇◇◇

art writing, inartistic (and often incomprehensible):
Writing about art is very often synonymous with wretched writing for one simple reason: It apparently attracts pretentious overblown writers the way shit attracts flies, if we may be so blunt. As such it usually winds up being an ostensibly impressive, overwhelming mass of polysyllables, tortured syntax, and words we rarely (if ever) hear. But all that tortured, pseudo-intellectual writing is actually a cover for ideas so utterly basic a third grader can understand them . . . as you will see when we translate the following examples of truly wretched art writing.

Untranslated Art Writing Example 1

I juxtapose anticipated with anomalous imagery to create visual analogies. Discrepancy and contrast in scale are emphasized as I investigate perception and memory.

—In a brochure for a show by
photographer Sura Ruth

Translation: I like to take pictures that have things you'd expect to see right next to things you wouldn't expect to see. I like to put big things next to little things in my pictures, too. And I think my pictures show us how we all see things and remember things.

Untranslated Art Writing Example 2

> In terms of arting, where the reference condition is not fixed or even known conceptually but rather something coming to being, what can we hope through our formative hermeneutic movement? To make the "otherness" of the arting process more other, more "objective" in a newer sense and less "subjective" in the older sense, so that the arting process itself speaks more purely?
>
> —Kenneth R. Beittel,
> "Formative Hermeneutics in the Arting Processes
> of an Other: The Philetics of Art Education,"
> *Art Education* (December 1974)

Translation: How do we figure out what art really is when a lot of times the art isn't finished but is still being made?

Untranslated Art Writing Example 3

> Post-modernism needs to be dealt with in the same manner as modernism, that is, as either exclusive or inclusive. The definition of exclusive post-modernism depends on a conception of exclusive modernism.

Exclusive post-modernism wants to invert exclusive modernism and, in the process, destroy it . . . Inclusive post-modernism is merely the latest stage of inclusive modernism, that is, modernism that encompasses post-modernism. Thus, both exclusive post-modernism and pluralism are opposed to exclusive modernism. But pluralism is broader than exclusive post-modernism, since it views art as open in every direction, including that of exclusive modernism.

—Irving Sandler,
in *Art Journal* (Fall/Winter 1980)

Translation (which really calls for pictures, preferably in color with happy faces. But text will have to do . . .): Let's look at art. There are many kinds of art today. There is art that is new, and there is art that isn't as new. There is art open to new ideas, and there is art that is closed to new ideas. So right now, let's meet our four different art types: Closed New Art, Open New Art, Closed Older Art, and Open Older Art. Oh, no. Look at Closed New Art. It is trying to hurt Closed Older Art. So are some Other People. The Other People like all different kinds of new ideas. But they don't like Closed Older Art, even though they are bigger. But Open New Art likes Open Older Art, because they are almost the same.

◇◇◇◇◇

autoeroticism: Autoerotic wretched writers seem to have a motto: "Let's put the 'auto' back in autoerotic writing." By this, they don't mean the "auto" as derived from the ancient Greek word for "self," as in "self-erotic," but a bit more prosaically: "auto" as in automobile. Like cars. As in sex and cars . . .

> She is topping up your engine oil for the cross-country coming up. Your RPM is hitting a new high. To wait any longer would be to lose prime time . . . She picks up a Bugatti's momentum. You want her more at a Volkswagen's steady trot. Squeeze the maximum mileage out of your gallon of gas. But she's eating up the road with all cylinders blazing.
> —Aniruddha Bahal, *Bunker 13* (2003)

Why stop with cars? There's always your basic engineering sexual imagery.

> More interesting to Whaleman were the fantastic breastworks, huge swollen globes of shiny flesh upon her chest, crowned with soft pink suckler tips—no doubt, the Gunner surmised—the mammary evidence of a runaway GPC maternal code. He realized that he was inspecting her with excessive interest but could not help himself. The mammala [*sic*] were exquisitely formed, curiously hard-soft in appearance, and jutting out from the chest in a manner that aroused Whaleman's engineering curiosity.
> —Don Pendleton, *The Guns of Terra 10* (1974)

And some intrepid wretched writers go even further than that.

They boldly go where no man has gone before, to the ultimate: spaceship sexual imagery.

> Though the multiple kisses Kirk was deploying along the length of the body beneath him were going off like very tiny photon torpedoes . . .
> —Alan Dean Foster,
> *Star Trek* (based on the screenplay by
> Roberto Orci and Alex Kurtzman) (2009)

Which leaves us with a question: Did Captain Kirk succeed in firing his large photon torpedo at the end of the chapter?

backing into things: The best way to do almost anything is to begin at the beginning, and move on from there. This tends to be true in writing sentences as well—a good sentence begins with a basic idea and proceeds from there. But there are always some bold intrepid writers with a creative streak who emulate the mythical Kansas jayhawk (more on said bird below) and say to themselves, "Hey, what if I write a sentence sort of backward; you know, begin in the middle or the end and proceed from there instead?"

Unfortunately, the results are not pretty.

> Like the mythical Kansas jayhawk, that bird which flew backwards—it didn't care where it was going but

it certainly wanted to know where it had been—
Wesley David Cardigan awoke the next day in his
room at the State House, deeply perplexed.

—Lee David Willoughby, *The Gunfighters* (1981)

◇

Since it had been brought by her so belatedly with
respect to his departure, use it Barry Wayne had not
even bothered to do, for fully dressed he already had
been by then—and combed, as well, through the
sense of feel also, had been his hair.

—Harry Stephen Keeler,
The Monocled Monster (1947)

body parts and bodily fluids, peripatetic (see also anatomy, problematic): Some body parts—like arms, legs, and fingers—are expected to move. But outside of horror or surrealistic novels, other body parts are expected to stay where they belong. In the hands of some writers, however, these body parts break free and stroll, slither, or hurl themselves about. To wit:

Starr's hands were going numb and his arms were
drifting slowly away from their sockets.

—Peter Heath, *Men Who Die Twice* (1968)

◇

[The chair] rocked briefly in his absence, then stead-
ied to await the next set of perambulating buttocks.
> —Alan Dean Foster, *Diuturnity's Dawn* (2002)

◇

His mouth, for a moment, ran liquid and then it slid,
almost of its own accord, down his throat.
> —Isaac Asimov, *Prelude to Foundation* (1988)

◇

The blood that had abandoned her countenance
rushed into his.
> —Elizabeth Peters, *Lion in the Valley:*
> *An Amelia Peabody Mystery* (1986)

Sometimes the body parts don't move of their own volition,
but they are movable—or removable—when they shouldn't be:

She threw her face over her apron.
> —Charles Reade,
> *The Cloister and the Hearth* (1861)

◇

After peeling off her long, shapely legs, she straight-
ened and stretched her nude body luxuriously.
> —Adam Coulter, *Debauchee* (1963)

◇

She wanted to pick her heart up like a naughty toddler and take it outside and smack it until it stopped leaping about like this.

—Gillian White, *The Plague Stone* (1996)

◇

Kothar leaped, leaving his booted feet and diving a yard above the floor.

—Gardner F. Fox,
Kothar: Barbarian Swordsman (1969)

◇

His feet slammed into Alayn's knees and knocked them both to the floor.

—Katharine Kerr, *Snare* (2003)

And then there are body parts that actually are able to move but shouldn't—or if they do, we as readers would prefer not to know.

Even Ilona's asshole has been puckered for the camera; it gives us a knowing wink, demanding our complicity.

—Adrian Searle,
"Pop Life's Schlock Horrors," *The Guardian*
(September 29, 2009)

◇◇◇◇◇

book titles, boring: The astute author knows that a book title must be catchy, riveting, or otherwise compelling. Sometimes this rule is violated, perhaps owing to less-than-catchy, non-riveting, or otherwise-uncompelling-to-the-masses topic choice. To wit:

Greek Rural Postmen and Their Cancellation Numbers, **by Derek Willan (1994)**

> Lists virtually *all* rural cancellation numbers used in the Greek postal system. (Related works include the *Illustrated Ottoman Turkish Postmarks 1840–1929* and *Postal Rates in Iceland 1870–1997.*)

Highlights in the History of Concrete, **by C. C. Stanley (1979, Rev. 1994)**

> Probably one of the most gripping books ever published by the British Cement Association.

The History and Romance of Elastic Webbing, **by Clifford A. Richmond (1946)**

> A passionately felt history of the rise of elastic webbing in the critical years of the nineteenth century.

According to the author, once a man has "got the smell of rubber in his nostrils . . . he either stays with rubber or is thereafter ever homesick to get back into the rubber industry." We are sure he is correct.

Parish Minister's Hats, by James Martin (1997)

Unfortunately limited to the hats of Reformed and Presbyterian denominations.

The Romance of Cement, by the Edison Portland Cement Company (1926)

Another entry in the surprisingly large concrete/cement book category. From the company that invented the ill-fated single piece cast concrete suburban house (prone to leaks) and popularized the idea of cement pianos.

A Study of Hospital Waiting Lists in Cardiff, 1953–1954, by Ernest Lewis-Faning, Fred Grundy, and Robert Arthur Nauton Hitchens (1956)

Answers the question: What happened to the over 20,000 people on Cardiff Hospital waiting lists? The short answer: Most were admitted.

[Ed. note: Others felt better, and thus took their names off the list; and 126 individuals were unaware they even were on a hospital waiting list. In Cardiff.]

Who's Who in Barbed Wire, by Rabbit Ear Publishing Co. (1970)

The go-to volume for information on the barbed wire collecting community.

◇◇◇◇◇

book titles, not-so-boring: Other book titles are far from boring, but also are inadvertently problematic due their un-boringness. We refer to those (typically from years gone by) that conjure up rather inappropriate images, images we doubt the author had in mind. Herewith the Top 13 Excessively Interesting and Inappropriately Imagistic Book Titles:

The Big Problem of Small Organs, by Alan T. Kitley (1966)
Biggles Takes It Rough, by W. E. Johns (1963)
Dildo Cay, by Nelson Hayes (1940)
Drummer Dick's Discharge, by Beatrix M. De Burgh (1902)
How Nell Scored, by Bessie Marchant (1929)
Invisible Dick, by Frank Topham (1926)
Memorable Balls, by James Laver (1954)
Muffs and Morals, by Pearl Binder (1955)

Scouts in Bondage, by Geoffrey Prout (1930)

Simple Hints for Mothers on the Home Sex-Training of Boys, by Clare Goslett (1914)

Sloppy Dingle, by Percy Curtiss (1874)

Warne's Pleasure Book for Boys, ed. W. J. Gordon (1933)

Why Bring That Up? A Guide to and from Seasickness, by Dr. J. F. Montague (1936)

<><><><><>

breasts, strange: Herewith we examine a very specific offshoot of the anatomically troubled school of wretched writing. We speak of the breast (female). The female breast is often a problematic body part for writers. Eager to give breasts their due but also eager to sidestep the typical descriptions, many writers feel compelled to imbue them with unique, indeed odd, qualities that are not normally found in the typical human breast. Thus the reader encounters a myriad of strange breasts. There are . . .

Breasts That Are Like Things That Are Not at All Breast-Like

Beneath the contour jewellery her breasts lay like eager snakes.

—J. G. Ballard,
"The Cloud-Sculptors of Coral D" (1967)

[Ed. note: We are especially impressed with this line not only because breasts are not often thought of as snakelike—there are other body parts that more often get the "snake" treatment, although women don't have said parts—but also because we rarely think of snakes as particularly eager.]

If Dawn Madden's breasts were a pair of Danishes, Debby Crombie's got two Space Hoppers. Each armed with a gribbly nipple.
—David Mitchell, *Black Swan Green* (2006)

[Ed. note: Mitchell gets extra points for making up a word.]

Jocelyn came through the fog wall, muttering, her breasts swaying like two angry red eyes looking for a fight.
—Gregory Benford, *Furious Gulf* (1994)

Breasts That Do Things Breasts Typically Don't Do

Her hips were beautifully arched and her breasts were like proud flags waving triumphantly.
—Michael Avallone,
The Case of the Violent Virgin (1957)

◇

Her breasts were twin mounds of female muscle that quivered and hung and quivered and hung again.
—Michael Avallone,
The Crazy Mixed-Up Corpse (1957)

◇

Her breasts weren't only round and full. They pulsed and throbbed like living perfections.

—Michael Avallone,
The Crazy Mixed-Up Corpse (1957)

◇

Suddenly Kris had boobs. Boobs that she knew all too well how to make go boom.

—Mike Shepherd, *Kris Longknife: Audacious* (2007)

Breasts That Have Strangely Behaving Nipples

Her slender chest rose and fell gently and slowly with her sleeping inhalations, her small breasts and rather larger nipples outdenting the flimsy fabric of her ragged tunic . . .

—Fritz Leiber,
The Knight and Knave of Swords (1988)

◇

Our teeth grated, and my nipples went *spung*!

—Robert Heinlein, *The Number of the Beast* (1986)

◇

Even through two layers of combat armour, I felt her nipples brush against my back . . .

—Karl Hansen, *War Games* (1981)

[Ed. note: We can't help wondering just what kind of weapons-grade nipples are these?]

She ferociously massaged her own breasts, and the nipples rose like pink silos bursting with harvested emotions.

—Louis Fisher, *Wild Party* (1960)

bureaucratese: Bureaucratese is very specific type of wretched writing churned out by the government and corporate staffers who wile away their working hours writing memos, directives, missives, announcements, presentations, articles, etc. Said staffers make said memos, directives, missives, etc., change alchemically from plain English to painful bureaucratese by mastering a number of arcane arts:

Saying Absolutely Nothing About Something

No unmet needs exist and . . . current unmet needs that are being met will continue to be met.

—Transportation Commission
on Unmet Transit Needs,
Mariposa County, California

Taking Something Very Simple (Say, Taking a Day Off of Work or Changing Your Flight) and Making It Mind-Bogglingly Complicated

Charges for changes and cancellations
Note—cancellations—before departure fare is refundable. If combining a non-refundable fare with a refundable fare only the y/c/j-class half return amount can be refunded. After departure fare is refundable. If combining a non-refundable fare with a refundable fare refund the difference/if any/between the fare paid and the applicable normal BA oneway fare. Changes/upgrades—permitted anytime.

> —British Airways notice on cancellation terms

Specifying Absolutely Nothing

Tenses, Gender, and Number: For the purpose of the rules and regulations contained in this chapter, the present tense includes the past and future tenses, and the future, the present; the masculine gender includes the feminine, and the feminine, the masculine, and the singular includes the plural, and the plural the singular.

> —In the state code for the Department of Consumer Affairs, California

Bold, Indeed Obvious, Repetition

TABLE 3.7: Average monthly income receivers income and percentage of income receivers by income receivers income and percentage income receivers and sector.

—Title of chart sent to the US-AID
by the government of Sri Lanka

◇◇◇◇◇

cacophony, catastrophic (or When Sound Effects Attack): In an effort to make a scene come alive, many writers use words to imitate a sound like a phone ringing ("brringg") or a pigeon cooing ("coo") or a gun firing ("bang"). The technical term for this is "onomatopoeia." Because that is so difficult to spell, we herein will refer to it as simply "sound effect."

When it comes to wretched writing, some intrepid writers eschew the ever-so-obvious "brringg," "coo," or "bang." It is this creative aural attitude that gives us truly unique, yet extraordinarily bizarre, literary sound effects.

"Grrrrrr," said the telephone.
"Can you speak up?" Fear had enveloped the girl.
"Grr, er ur arr," said the telephone again.
Lana held it away from her as though it was a
    supernatural monster.

"Who are you? What are you?"

"Grr, rrr, arrr, spptttzzz," said the telephone.

—John E. Muller (Lionel Fanthorpe),
Spectre of Darkness (1965)

◇

Hyueeps, Hyueeps, Hyueeps, Oho!

Out, my pretties! Ho! my pretties!

Cooing, cooing love and ditties!

—Théophile Marzials,
"The Gallery of Pigeons" (1873)

◇

Against a backdrop of darkness the heater sneezed:
KA-CHOWP! CHOWP! CHOWP! And sent three
sparking ribbons of orange flame burning into the
pillow.

—Robert Leslie Bellem,
"Come Die for Me" (1946)

This take on the sound of a steam engine deserves special
mention for not reminding one of an engine at all. It somehow
reminds us more of . . . eating crackers in a bathtub.

The engine pants and snorts and blows
The carriage doorways slam and close
The broad and ponderous wheels are rolled
By thick-set arms of iron mould,
While streaming from the spouting side
The steam escapes in hissing tide.

Cranch, crunch, thud, rud, duvver-duh-ruh,
Thudder, rubber, dub-dub, dub-a-ruh-ruh-ruh.

> —Rev. Edward Dalton,
> "The Railway Journey" (fl. 1860s)

Sometimes the bad sound effects come not from inanimate objects but from people.

[She] finally came to him in the bed and shouted "Ar-ragghrrorwr!" in his ear, bit his neck, plunged her head between his legs and devoured him.

> —William Safire, *Full Disclosure* (1977)

◇

"Bluh!" he choked. "Ahk! Bluh!"
"Caw!" the cop said urgently. "Caw! Fuh! Bah-up!"

> —Stephen King, *Rose Madder* (1996)

Our reaction to all of this? Arragghrrorwr! Or rather, Ahk! Bluh!

◇◇◇◇◇

cacophony, overdoing it/enough already: In other cases of wretched writing, the problem is not the sound effect itself, but the enthusiastic overuse of the sound. Here the word "cacophony"—from the ancient Greek, meaning (to somewhat oversimplify) "bad" (*caca*) "sound" (*phony*)—calls to us. For example, in the following, the reader (or listener) understands that this is a bell ringing. But this bell never *stops* ringing—over and over and over and over . . . One is reminded of a not-wretched writer, Edgar Allan Poe, who treated this subject a bit differently (which is to say better) in his poem "The Bells."

> Ring, ingle, dang, dong,
> My hard iron song
> In the old belfry sung.
> Dong, dangle, ring, ding,
> With flustering wing
> Sped by each iron tongue . . .
> Ring, ding, ding, ring, ring, ding, dang, dong.
> Ring, ding, dang, dong.
> Ding, dang, dong.
> Dang, dong.
> D-O-N-G.

—William Nathan Stedman,
"The Man in the Moon" (1907)

Speaking of dongs, even more annoying are those found in "The Sun of My Songs," by the eccentric poet and composer Théophile Marzials.

> Yet all your song
> Is—"Ding, dong,"
> Summer is dead,
> Spring is dead—
> O my heart, and O my head!
> Go a-singing a silling song,
> All wrong,

For all is dead,
   Ding, dong,
And I am dead,
Dong!

—Théophile Marzials,
"The Sun of My Songs" (1873)

◇◇◇◇◇

cacophony, tepid: One final word on sound effects in wretched writing: Sometimes (but oh so rarely) instead of overdoing it, the wretched writer underdoes it, as in this less than exciting scene:

> Now with all eight of his people on one swamprunner, West needed help and the *Halicarnassus* was about to provide it. Two missiles lanced out from its belly-pods, missing one Apache by inches, but hitting the one behind it.
> Boom. Fireball.
> —Matthew Reilly, *Seven Ancient Wonders* (2005)

Boom. We are underwhelmed.

◇◇◇◇◇

celebrity novelists: The celebrity novel (i.e., a novel written by a person known as a celebrity) is a specific type of wretched writing that has become more popular—and lucrative—than ever. It has, of course, a distinguished literary history. Upon examination of this burgeoning field of literature, one can see that there is absolutely no truth to the rumor that publishing companies purchase said novels purely for sales potential and not for literary merit. The following examples will bear this out:

Pamela Anderson, *Star: A Novel* (2004)

Ms. Anderson, if not well known for her brain, is quite well known for the other (two) bumps of her anatomy. Her literary corpus (appropriately, *two* novels) naturally seems to focus on those large and fleshy protuberances (of which, of course, there are *two*). The cover flap from her debut novel, *Star,* essentially sums up the interior content and general literary quality perfectly: "What really happens when A-list meets D-cup?" A pertinent question.

Excerpt

"Honey," Lucille said, stroking her daughter's hair. "What's wrong?"

"I . . . I found . . . a lump," Star managed to choke out.

"A lump?" Lucille asked, confused.

"Right here." Star took her mother's hand and placed in on the poisonous node. "I think it's cancer."

"Oh," Lucille said, drawing back suddenly and laughing as she wrapped her arms around her beloved daughter. "Well, well, well," she said, rocking

Star gently. "You're not dying, you're just growing up. Looks like you're finally going to get some boobs. You're becoming a woman, honey. You're blooming!"

And bloom she did. Her breasts came on suddenly and tenaciously, as if trying to make up for lost time. The hard bump turned out to be one of a pair of unruly and self-willed nipples.

[Ed. note: "Unruly nipples"?]

Naomi Campbell, *Swan* (1996)

Ms. Campbell's designation as a celebrity novelist is somewhat unusual if only because Campbell's agent actually admitted Naomi didn't exactly write the story of a model's life in her own words. Instead, she sort of wrote it. If you are confused, so are we. In the agent's words: "Naomi's very much the author but Caroline [Upcher] is the writer. That's fair. You can't expect Naomi to produce a novel straight off on her own." Maybe you can't. Who are we to quarrel with such a celebrity?

Excerpt from *Swan*

Sprawled in front of a spin drier, wearing nothing but a pair of white cotton briefs and sneakers, her cropped hair thrown back as she chugalugged a can of Diet Coke, her pierced nose with the chain stretched across her face and running down her lip, Celestia came across on the page as an unmistakably classy piece of ass.

Nicole "Snooki" Polizzi, *A Shore Thing* (2010)

Following in the footsteps of fellow "novelist" Naomi Campbell, celebrity author Snooki also engaged another author to do the tedious duty of actually setting pen to paper. We suspect her reason relates more to basic illiteracy than time constraints, but we speculate.

Excerpt

> Gia danced around a little, shaking her peaches for show. She shook it hard. Too hard. In the middle of a shimmy, her stomach cramped. A fart slipped out. A loud one. And stinky.

[Ed. note: A tip of the hat to Balzacian naturalism.]

celebrity poets (see also rhymes, facile, page 167): Some celebrity writers prefer to turn their writing "talents" to versification rather than fiction writing. The result is often charmingly puerile . . .

Leonard Nimoy, aka Mr. Spock, went where no star had gone

before in penning a series of poetry books and offered us a less than startling study of stardom and fame and observes that:

> You're hit with a spotlight from above
> Your fans are screaming words of love
> —Leonard Nimoy, "Pictures of You" (2011)

Some celebrity poets get run over by bad metaphors:

> I draw a hot sorrow bath in my despair room.
> —Keanu Reeves,
> "Ode to Happiness," *Ode to Happiness*, 2011

And others—like Charlie Sheen—try a bit too hard to sound poetically intellectual and shocking—and they end up sounding (sadly) like Charlie Sheen.

> Vaginal riots in the Middle East
> Do I have a choice? Do I have an option?
> Mommy, I love you
> —Charlie Sheen, "A Tale of Two Sisters" (1989)

character descriptions, too much: Here is yet another example of how many wretched writers are doomed by love of excess descriptive information—in this case, specifically about their beloved characters. In their zeal to make these characters come

alive and seem real to the reader, these writers go overboard—
and in a generously large way offer a veritable deluge of descriptive information about their characters. Too much information. A
cornucopia of information.

While laudably generous, throwing hundreds of descriptive
words of character description is not a particularly good way of
encouraging a reader to read on and find out more. For example
in *Bronwyn, Silk and Steel*, we learn virtually *everything* there
is to know about Bronwyn, the main character, in one go. (Or
rather, almost everything. Her spleen curiously is not mentioned.)

> Her hair had the sheen of the sea beneath an eclipsed
> moon. It was the color of a leopard's tongue, of oiled
> mahogany. It was terra cotta, bay and chestnut. Her
> hair was a helmet, a hood, the cowl of the monk,
> magician or cobra.
>
> Her face had the fragrance of a gibbous moon.
> The scent of fresh snow. Her eyes were dark birds in
> fresh snow. They were the birds' shadows, they were
> mirrors; they were the legends on old charts. They
> were antique armor and the tears of dragons. Her
> brows were a raptor's sharp, anxious wings. They
> were a pair of scythes. Her ears were a puzzle
> carved in ivory. Her teeth were her only bracelet; she
> carried them within the red velvet purse of her lips.
> Her tongue was amber. Her tongue was a ferret, an
> anemone, a fox caught in the teeth of a tiger.
>
> Her shoulders were the clay in a potter's kiln. Her
> shoulders were fieldstones; they were the white,
> square stones of which walls are made. They were

windows covered with steam. They were porcelain. They were opal and moonstone. Her neck was the foam that curls from the prow of a ship, it was a sheaf of alfalfa or barley, it was the lonely dance of the pearl-grey shark.

Her legs were quills. They were bundles of wicker, they were candelabra; the muscles were summer lightning, that flickered like a passing thought; they were captured eels . . .

—Ron Miller, *Bronwyn, Silk and Steel* (1992)

[Ed. note: In deference to your tolerance level, we have spared you the descriptions of Brownyn's thighs, calves, feet, toes, arms, fingers, spine, buttocks, breasts, nipples, ribs, stomach, and pubic hair.]

If you are still awake, let us now introduce one of Bronwyn's older sisters-in-excess. While this character, Elsa Colby, was created many years before, she is just as overdescribed and boring as Bronwyn.

The bright red of Elsa's hair—made even brighter, seemingly, by its contrast with the knitted mouse-grey one-piece dress that she wore—was of the exact color as the great scarlet poppies which lay at each corner of the quilt; her blue eyes were precisely the blue of the pond which lay at its middle—at least of the one experimentally completed ripple on that pond; and the freckles on her face—and most particularly on her nose—were like—but no, they were not like anything on the quilt proper at all, but were like the spattering of brown ink from an angry fountain-pen on a sheet of white paper. Her quilt, it might be said, lay exposed in entirety upon its huge rack for the simple reason that it held, here and there, throughout its entire area, certain flecks which must be done in green; and Elsa, having been able to pick up a huge amount of green silk thread—but green only!—at a discount, had to do that color first, and fully, just as independent shoestring movie producers, with little or no money to rent locations or put up settings, have to complete, in one rented setting, all the scenes for two or more "quickies,"—before negotiating a new setting!

—Harry Stephen Keeler,
The Man with the Wooden Spectacles (1941)

character intros, wretchedly bad: The first several seconds of a job interview, the experts say, are crucial. It is in those seconds that the job interviewer makes a basic decision about the suitability of the job candidate.

Similarly the first few lines of a character introduction, when the author tells us something about the characters in his or her novel, are crucial. Here the reader decides whether to read on— or to throw the book with vigor across the room. Following are the two short character introductions from novels which make our throwing arms most itchy:

Redwayne TerVyne, known to the Chinese of America, because of his passion for Chinese items in his nationally syndicated column, as "The Great White Prynose," and to New York in general as "The Keyhole," hopped out of his luxurious $10,000 purple car in front of the row of de luxe art shops on Fifth Avenue.

—Harry Stephen Keeler,
The Strange Will (1948)

A door closed, and the Italian Girl, Maria, the short gray-haired woman who decades ago had replaced the famous Helen Day, called the Cup Bearer, at other times referred to more mysteriously as O'Dotto, came out of Daisy's studio carrying an empty tray.

—Peter Straub, *The Hellfire Club* (1995)

clauses, confusing: Clauses—little snippets of complete ideas that appear in the middle of sentences—can be used to expand an idea, to clarify, to limit, or to otherwise modify the sentence.

Or in the hands of a wretched writer, they can completely baffle, confuse, bore, and otherwise irritate the reader.

East or West, it matters not where—the story may, doubtless, indicate something of the latitude and longitude as it proceeds—in the city of Mishaumok, lived Henderson Gartney, Esq., one of those American gentlemen of whom, if she were ever canonized, Martha of Bethany must be the patron saint—if again, feminine celestials, sainthood once achieved through the weary experience of earth, don't know better than to assume such charge of wayward man—born, as they are, seemingly, to the life-destiny of being ever "careful and troubled about many things."

—Adeline Dutton Whitney,
Faith Gartney's Girlhood (1863)

◇

Now he understood how the great, unlettered military genius Genghis Khan, as well as the illiterate or semi-literate military leaders of peoples such as the Quanrong, the Huns, the Tungus, the Turks, the Mongols, and the Jurchens, were able to bring the Chinese (whose great military sage Sun-tzu had produced his universally acclaimed treatise *The Art of War*) to their knees, to run roughshod over their territory, and to interrupt their dynastic cycles.

—Jiang Rong, *Wolf Totem* (2008)

When a writer throws in too many clauses, the reader gets tangled in a net of asides and extraneous thoughts—and winds up losing track of whatever the hell the writer was talking about in the first place.

Part of a series called "Living Architectures"—which includes "Gehry's Vertigo," a trip on the roofs of Frank

---

Gehry's Guggenheim Museum in Bilbao—by Ila Bêka and Louise Lemoine, a husband-and-wife team of filmmakers, *Koolhaas Houselife* deals with the "afterlife" of the widely published and highly praised house near Bordeaux, France, built by Rem Koolhaas of the Dutch architecture firm OMA for the family of a successful publisher, Jean-François Lemoine, confined to a wheelchair when his life was permanently altered by a crippling automobile accident.

—Ada Louise Huxtable,
"Ingenious and Demanding,"
The Wall Street Journal (September 30, 2009)

And keeping a sentence somewhat short doesn't help when a confusing clause is perfectly (which is to say irritatingly) inserted:

The young pinch-faced hombre and girl, bathed in the scintillating sunlight that touched the jeweled valleys of the sparkling basin beneath the frowning line of the distant hills beyond the rangeland, made an incongruous pair.

—Will Garth, *Lawless Guns* (1937)

◇

"We're going to clean up your act and send you out looking like a princess," a pretty dark-haired eastern European called Xheni who had recently been scouted by one of the top model agencies assured her.

—Susan Stephens, *Maharaja's Mistress* (2011)

clichés, mangled: Wretched writers often take good honest overused clichés and crush them in their literary vises. The results are not new clichés, because no one in their right mind would reuse them. Let's call them one-time-only mangled clichés, which means they're not really clichés anymore, are they? Oh, never mind.

Sometimes we can clearly see where the author went wrong:

> Labor interests may be cutting off their nose despite their face.
>
> —Rep. Nick Smith,
> (R-MI), congressional press release

◇

> But when the boom went bust, the golden goose still ruled the roost.
>
> —Sarah Palin,
> *Going Rogue: An American Life* (2009)

Sometimes the author seems to sense there's a problem, and tries (unsuccessfully) to throw in another line to clarify things. Instead we get zombie deer.

> They turned around like deer in the headlights. Deer who had also been shot.
>
> —William F. Weld, *Mackerel by Moonlight* (1998)

Sometimes the cliché gets wrapped up in another, and then we get things like diplomats under tables with maps like umbrellas. Or something.

> [Sharon] gave an ultimatum to the Palestinians: either come to the negotiating table under the umbrella of the road map to peace or face unilateral action by Israel.
>
> —Ewen MacAskill,
> "Sharon Ready to Sacrifice Some Jewish Outposts,"
> *The Guardian* (December 19, 2003)

◇◇◇◇◇

clichés, overused: It can be difficult to avoid the hackneyed, the trite, and the overused cliché when writing. But avoid one must try—lest one fall into the habit of tossing off prose in which people are *comfortable in their own skin*, when they get shocked, they are *riveted by shock*, and when they go to sleep, they always *sleep like the dead*.

Needless to say, some writers (shall we guess what type?) fail at this attempt.

> He came one morning when the sun was a molten mass of hell in the brassy sky, and it took only one look at him. Trouble—with a capital "T."
>
> —Brad Ward, *The Spell of the Desert* (1951)

◇

> There is a small patch of land in New York City that
> may have more symbolic meaning of what is America
> than any other place. Deep in the frenetic canyons of
> capitalism, surrounded by glass and concrete and steel
> that is the framework of the towering structures known
> as Wall Street, nothing ever is what it appears to be.
>
> —Peter Thomas Senese,
> *The Den of the Assassin* (2012)

In fairness to Mr. Senese, we must point out that it is not only *his* prose that is replete with clichés, but also that of whoever writes his jacket copy—in which we run through a veritable gauntlet of clichés. We have helpfully bolded said clichés in the copy for his *Chasing the Cyclone* (2011):

> Except Paul has one problem: he lives with a **deep dark secret** that torments him: he is a ghost living in purgatory despite his relative wealth and success. Unknown to Paul, there is an evil plan to extort his **hard-earned assets** from him and in the process **deny him the one thing that is more important to him than anything else in the world**: to be an active part of his son Alex's life. Unfortunately, **his innocent and trusting seven-year-old son** is at the center of this **vicious and diabolical plot** directed at him. When **things go from bad to worse to unbelievably insane**—when judges choose not to uphold the laws of their nations, when **law enforcement turns a blind eye**, and when one government after

another's hands are tied due to bureaucratic issues of jurisdiction or non-participation of the international treaty on child abduction, the only thing that could prevent Alex from becoming another **sad and sorry statistic** on a report that nobody wants to read or think about is his **father's vow to never abandon** him no matter what.

It's enough to make us want to belly up to the bar, drown our sorrows in drink, and tear our hair out in frustration.

◇◇◇◇◇

clumsiness: Some wretched writing defies simple categorization. Thus the catch-all category "clumsy." The problem with the writing in this category isn't necessarily syntax or overuse of literary device or mixed metaphor. It's sometimes more than that—and sometimes less than that . . . and sometimes both. It thunks on the ear or thuds on the page. For whatever reason, it's clumsy. Catastrophically so.

> Beams and timbers of misery and wanting clashed within me.
>
> —John Norman, *Raiders of Gor* (1971)

◇

> Judging by their elephant-sized jewels they had turned out to honor one man—though it was the people who were the jewels of Ram's country . . .
>
> —Susan Stephens, *Maharaja's Mistress* (2011)

◇

"What is it, Arthur?" Admiral Greer asked, wearing a cheap golf shirt.

—Tom Clancy, *Red Rabbit* (2002)

[Ed. note: Why the shirt, Tom? And why there? Tom?]

The walls had fallen down and the Windows had opened, making the world much flatter than it had ever been—but the age of seamless global communication had not yet dawned.

—Thomas Friedman, *The World Is Flat* (2005)

[Ed. note: Opening a window in a fallen wall makes the world flat? Which links to seamless global communication?]

"Let me out of here!" blubbered the man, wheeling like a fish out of water to his right.

—Tom Roan, *Gun Lord of Silver River* (1943)

[Ed. note: Blubbering man + right-wheeling fish = crying readers.]

Her interest was as pointed as the breasts on which she gently splashed cold water.

—Robert Holdstock, *Merlin's Wood* (1994)

[Ed. note: This is a simile, and a pretty bad one at that. But it also seems as though the breasts are rather gratuitous—which earns its special clumsy rating.]

◇◇◇◇◇

colorful language, excessive 1: A subset of the "excessive adjective school of wretched writing," in this case the culprit is specifically addicted to using colors in his or her descriptions. Of course, it is fine to describe things by what color they are—the blue car, the red book, etc. It is sometimes even better to go into a little more detail—"the bruise turned various shades of purple and green," etc. But these are what we call "paint pot" writers who blithely splash a Technicolor nightmare onto the page.

> Sunset blazed above the Guadalupes like the spilled paint pots of a drunken artist-god. Orange and gold and scarlet and damask was the flaming background, with highlights of salmon and rose and chrome. Patches of sky like rain-streaked steel showed here and there, their ragged edges tinted faintly as with powdered verd. Shafts of amber lanced to the zenith, paling and thinning until they vanished in the higher blue.
>
> —Jackson Cole,
> *Riders of the Rimrock Trail* (1942)

Sometimes there are so many colors the writer himself gets confused. What color *is* that rock anyway?

There were pinkish streaks among the rock, and it seemed that the chromatic tint from the atmosphere owed something to these. There were a number of white veins in the rock, which bore some resemblance to marble, but the majority of it was grey. It gave an over-all impression of greyness streaked with pink and white, rather than an over-all impression of whiteness tinged with grey and pink, or an over-all impression of pink streaked with grey and white. Greyness was the predominant shade; neither black nor white but something midway between the two . . .

—Pel Torro (Lionel Fanthorpe),
Galaxy 666 (1968)

[Ed. note: And who effing cares? It's a ROCK.]

⬦⬦⬦⬦⬦

colorful language, excessive 2: There is another form of colorful language that can pose problems in writing. We speak, of course, of profanity. Or more bluntly, your "shits," your "fucks," and your otherwises. In some instances, a little profanity, like a pinch of salt or pepper, adds seasoning and a touch of verisimilitude or color to a novel. And in some cases, even a lot may make a character seem more realistic and vivid. But sometimes it can get to be a little fucking too much, as in these selections from a single chapter (Chapter 14) in Michael Crichton's novel *Prey*.

"Jesus fucking A," Charley muttered . . . Charley mouthed something to me. I thought he mouthed, "That fucking guy wants us killed." . . . "Form up in two rows!" Charley grabbed the Windex spray bottle and fell into line, grumbling, "What do you think our fucking chances are?" . . . Between claps, Charley said, "Do you believe—this fucking shit—it's working!" . . . I heard Charley whisper "Oh fuck," under his breath, . . . "Come on, Jack," Charley said. "Let's get the fuck out of here." . . . Charley grabbed her shoulder and said, "God damn it, Rosie—"

"Fuck you!" She wrenched free from his grip . . . Charley leaned close to me and said, "It's not your fucking fault." . . . "Oh fuck," Charley said . . . I think we're fucked," Charley said . . . "Yow!" he said. "Fucking hot!" . . . "What fucking difference does it make?" Charley said. "We're in two of the fucking cars, Ricky." . . .

"It's not like the shed. These cars are airtight. So . . . fuck 'em." . . . "Yeah, I see it. Fuck a duck." . . . "Fuck these guys." . . . "Ah fuck. What's the point?" . . . We heard his voice from the black interior. "Yeah, okay . . . I'm looking—can't find—fucking door handle . . ."

—Michael Crichton, *Prey* (2002)

Then there are those times when the writer is trying a bit hard to shock but ends up simply boring the reader. In our view, seventeen fucks are sixteen fucks too many, and as for a whole page . . .

> Dear Dad, Fuck Fuck Fuck Fuck Fuck Fuck Fuck Fuck
> Fuck Fuck Fuck Fuck Fuck Fuck Fuck Fuck Fuck Fuck
> Fuck Fuck Fuck Fuck Fuck Fuck Fuck Fuck Fuck Fuck
> Fuck Fuck Fuck Fuck . . .
>
> —Macauley Culkin, *Junior* (2006)

On the other hand, sometimes one longs for a profane word or two:

> "My god, I married an animal!" Ralph said, disgust in his voice. "Can't you see you're a minister's wife?"
> "I'm beginning to see a lot of things, Ralph. One of which is I made a mistake . . . in marrying such a pompous wee-wee!"
>
> —William W. Johnstone,
> *Trail of the Mountain Man* (2000)

commas, problematic: Commas are small things that can cause big problems when a wretched writer is involved. The problem can result from an overenthusiastic sprinkling of commas, as if the writer had tossed a handful of raisins into their prose. This is sometimes called the "Shatner comma" after *Star Trek* actor William Shatner, because, it makes, the reader take, odd pauses, much like, William Shatner, acting, his lines.

Other times the problem is a missing comma—which can
wind up making an innocent phrase seem rather . . . salacious . . .
as in Bill Cosby's not-so-innocent-sounding book *Come On People*
and the children's masterpiece *Come On Mom.*

[*Ed. note: We have not read either book, but we assume that
the titular exhortations do not involve bodily emissions.*]

Then there's the problem that often arises with the so-called
Oxford comma. The Oxford comma is a comma used to separate
a series of ideas. It is not grammatically required, but if not used,
certain confusions can develop—as in the questionable hobbies
of a Nobel prize winner, the very questionable gender identification of two actors, and more.

◇

Among those interviewed were [singer Merle Hag-
gard's] two ex-wives, Kris Kristofferson and Robert
Duvall.

—Newspaper photo caption,
Los Angeles Times (July 21, 2010)

◇

The popular motels are used primarily by young people who live with their parents, prostitutes and adul-
terers.

—*International News*,
no. 163 (June 11, 1997)

◇◇◇◇◇

comprehensible topics, incomprehensibly written:
Sometimes writers get paid by the word. This is more often
the case with certain magazines and is not common in books.
But some writers seem to have embraced a "the more words
the better" trope and applied it to their writing with frighten-
ing results. In their (in)capable hands, a simple act—something
that could be described easily in, say, a four-word declara-
tive sentence—becomes many more words. Many, *many* more.

Here are some lengthy examples (with word counts) in as-
cending order, followed by the edited streamlined version.

52 Words

Hardly did he find himself within the enclosure than there were pressed upon him copious handfuls of grapes comprising a dozen or so large bunches, whereof he could not in civility refuse to accept a part, although unable to prevail on those hospitable vintagers to receive any acknowledgement of their courteous bounty.

—Algernon Taylor, *Guienne* (1879)

The revised 4-word version: He got free grapes.

94 Words

The move from a structuralist account in which capital is understood to structure social relationships in relatively homologous ways to a view of hegemony in which power relations are subject to repetition, convergence, and rearticulation brought the question of temporality into the thinking of structure, and marked a shift from a form of Althusserian theory that takes structural totalities as theoretical objects to one in which the insights into the contingent possibility of structure inaugurate a renewed conception of hegemony as bound up with the contingent sites and strategies of the rearticulation of power.

—Judith Butler, "Further Reflections on Conversations of Our Time," *Diacritics* 27, no. 1 (Spring 1997)

The revised ten-word version: Class systems are based on money, power, and social status.

188 Words (Algernon Taylor, Breaking His Own Record from Above)

To an observer of men and things Latin monasticism is chiefly interesting from a philosophical point of view, quite apart from the specialities of Romanist dogmas and practices, as the visible embodiment in these Western longitudes of the wide-spread monastic idea—an idea in which the East takes form and substance in the populist monasteries of Greek Christianity, and the yet more populist Buddhist conventual hives of both sexes. This idea, let it be ever so little realized in practice, is the same in each case. It is the spirit of retirement from an unsympathetic world that led the Psalmist and the Baptist alike to withdraw in the wilderness—"Lo, I fled, and got me far way: and dwelt in the wilderness"—and which, for more than two thousand years, has prompted many in all countries to follow their example, by exchanging the turmoil and ambitions of a gregarious life for the cloister—whether that cloister be Roman, Greek or Buddhist, or whether it represent the mildest of all forms of claustral life, the so-called Anglican Sisterhoods Brotherhoods of our own day and country.

—Algernon Taylor, *Guienne* (1879)

The revised eight-word version: People go to monasteries to escape the world.

◇◇◇◇◇

constructions, confusing, convoluted, and otherwise confounding: Some writers have a knack for this sort of wretched writing. They might use simple words or simple sentence construction, but the end product is something that is awe-inspiring in its obtuseness. We call this writing (logically) confusing, convoluted, or otherwise confounding because that's just what it is.

No matter how hard the reader tries to understand what he is reading, he can't.

[Ed. note: Well, we can't. Perhaps you are brighter than us.]

Tom Courtland was a talking man. And he didn't just talk words. He talked thoughts. And his thoughts were well worth thinking about no matter in whose head they were.

—John Fonville,
Where the Big Gun Rides (1961)

◇

He was not as old in appearance as his age might have made him appear.

—Gordon R. Dickson,
Soldier, Ask Not (1967)

They were both roughly the same age, in their very
early fifties, though a hundred years earlier they
would have appeared much younger.

—D. F. Jones, *Colossus* (1966)

◇

They forget (if they even can remember) the 1972
flight of Ugandan Indians from the brutal regime of Idi
Amin.

—Jonathan Coe,
Los Angeles Times Book Review (June 24, 2002)

◇

He pressed the button of the vibratory emulator; there
was an inaudible beam, a wavelength of death, a
movement that was less than a movement, and a motion that was less than a motion. And yet there were
movements and motions that were more than movements and motions.

—Karl Zeigfreid, *Android* (1962)

◇

Having had time to think it over, Andrew had decided
that he did not believe in this for a moment. If he had
not been so unfortunate at different times during the
last few years as to become involved in the solution

of a murder or two, so that he was more inclined than he would have been before he had been drawn into that rather gruesome activity to think that his own wild guesses were sometimes perhaps to be taken seriously, he would not even have considered such a possibility.

—E. X. Ferrars, *A Murder Too Many* (1989)

◇◇◇◇◇

creative comparisons, getting overly attached to: Many writers use analogies, metaphors, and similes (see pages 6, 128, and 177) in their work. Thus, we read of "too many fish in the sea" (when speaking of the dating pool as opposed to a school of flounder) or someone being "a rock" (when he is not actually gneiss—although he might be nice, ha ha . . .) and so forth.

And this is well and good, of course. However, many times writers also grow a teeny-weeny little bit too fond of whatever amazingly clever analogy they've come up with. They get carried away and can't stop piling it on—making the analogy or comparison an exhausting literary device indeed. In these cases, the analogy goes up in flames or inundates the reader . . .

To hell with warnings about playing with fire—it was too damn late for that. He'd not just played with fire—he'd set the bed ablaze! And it, and he, had gone up in a sheet of flame.

—Julia James,
The Greek's Million-Dollar Baby Bargain (2009)

◇

His words spluttered like a hose nozzle being adjusted, the stream of his conversation turned into a flood of apology.

—Lois Eby and John C. Fleming,
Death Begs the Question (1952)

◇◇◇◇◇

dangerous words, dated: In some cases, writing becomes wretched not necessarily because it was bad to begin with but because word meaning has changed. Thus a modern reader suddenly stumbles upon a phrase that, while innocent as the proverbial babe in the woods, now evokes an image that is not the one intended.

Take these rather, um, sticky situations with a formerly common synonym for the word "said":

"Shiver me timbers, but I'll dew suthin' with it," he ejaculated, holding up the missive and then feeling it over and over again.

—David Hickey,
William and Mary: A Tale of the Siege of Louisburg, 1745 (1884)

◇

"To think!" ejaculated the Lord de Vere, rather to himself than his companions, the best of whom he held
utterly unworthy of his intercourse . . .

—Nathaniel Hawthorne,
"The Great Carbuncle" (1837)

◇

Dr. Van Helsing rushed into the room, ejaculating
furiously.

—Bram Stoker, *Dracula* (1897)

◇

His landlady came to the door, loosely wrapped in
dressing-gown and shawl; her husband followed
ejaculating.

—H. G. Wells, *The War of the Worlds* (1898)

◇

"Oh!" ejaculated Bunter, with a jammy blink at the
crowd of juniors coming in. He had not expected an
audience. "I say, you fellows—"
    "Is he sticky?" asked the Bounder.

—Frank Richards, "The Tuck-Hoarder!" (1939)

We must also give a hand (so to speak) to the hero of early
ejaculation on the page: Captain W. E. Johns, author of the still-
beloved Biggles series. Biggles is an air ace and hero of the British
Empire from the 1930s on—who, along with his friends, seems

to spend less time flying and more time ejaculating—virtually everywhere. ("Great Scott!" ejaculated Biggles, "Good Lord!" ejaculated Bertie, "Ah ha!" ejaculated Biggles. Etc., etc., etc., etc.)

Then, of course, there's the problem with gay characters—because they aren't. Rather, not as we now commonly use the term (not that it would make any difference). Nevertheless, it can get quite confusing to suddenly get the feeling that the straightest of characters now apparently aren't.

This is what happens at the close of Kenneth Roberts's 1934 novel *Captain Caution*, which concludes with the captain's French friend *pinching another man's cheek* and cheerfully announcing that "I am gay again!"

We find other now queer-sounding references:

> I can only say with Mrs. March, "What *can* you expect when you have four gay girls in the house?"
> —Louisa May Alcott, *Little Women* (1868)

The First Chapter: Fag Wanted!

> "FAG!"
> Carberry, of the Sixth Form at Greyfriars, put his head out of his study and bawled along the passage.
> "Fag! F-a-a-g!"
> There was a faint sound of scurrying feet at the nearest corner, and then no other sound save the echo of Carberry's voice in the wide, flagged corridor upon which the Sixth Form studies opened.
> —Frank Richards, "The Taming of Harry" (1908)

dashes, overused: Dashes—what writer doesn't love 'em? Thomas Jefferson, Emily Dickinson, and many others just adored the things—and so do we.

But use them too much—and then you're writing wretchedly—since—as *New York Times* editor Phillip B. Corbett points out, they should be used "sparingly, and with care."

Not as in this *New York Times* article he found:

> Less romantic and—with instantly available pornography online and graphic sex talk, including on Mr. Hefner's own show, "The Girls Next Door," on TV—it's a time that makes Playboy's ideals seem quaint. Mr. Hefner—who uses the word "cat" to describe himself, as in, "I'm the luckiest cat on the planet"—doesn't think much of today's cultural landscape.
>
> —as quoted by Phillip B. Corbett
> in "Dashes Everywhere,"
> *The New York Times* (April 5, 2011)

But it gets much, much worse than that. As with one of our favorite wretched writers, Harry Stephen Keeler, who will make you wish to dash the book to the floor and dash out of the room. (Sorry.)

> And here was I—at 4:20 in the morning—with not less than the tail-end—if not the tail itself!—of certain information by which $100,000 might be made to change

hands—if and maybe, to be sure!—sitting in the office
of MacLeish MacPherson, M.D.!

—Harry Stephen Keeler,
The Mysterious Mr. I (1938)

◇◇◇◇◇

details, deadly: The timeworn cliché "the devil is in the details" may be taken literally in the case of prose written with a
passion-filled penchant for enlightening the reader with mind-
numbing, painfully dull ancillary facts.

How does a wretched writer make the end of the world and
the rise of the Antichrist boring? Simple. Ask Tim LaHaye, co-
author of *Left Behind* and creator of Global Community Supreme
Potentate and Antichrist Nicolae Carpathia (the Antichrist of
above), who is not exactly the most scintillating speech maker.

> "Our forebears were thinking globally long before I
> was born," Carpathia said. "In 1944, the year the
> International Monetary Fund and the World Bank
> were established, this great host nation, the United
> States of America, along with the British Common-
> wealth and the Union of Soviet Socialist Republics,
> met at the famous Dumbarton Oaks Conference to
> propose the birth of this body." Displaying his grasp
> of history and his photographic memory of dates and
> places, Carpathia intoned, "From its official birth on
> October 24, 1945, and that first meeting of your Gen-
> eral Assembly in London, January 10, 1946, to this

day, tribes and nations have come together to pledge their wholehearted commitment to peace, brotherhood and the global community."

—Tim LaHaye and Jerry B. Jenkins,
Left Behind (1995)

But Tim LaHaye's prose is spare and lean when compared to that of the infamous novelist and prolix word wielder Edward Bulwer-Lytton. Take a look at this passage, where we the readers are trying to meet an ancient character Glaucus. Instead of letting us, the writer subjects to us a long and stultifying exposition on the architecture of the Roman house. "We shall endeavor to make this description as clear and unpedantic as possible," he writes. He fails.

You enter then, usually, by a small entrance-passage (called cestibulum), into a hall, sometimes with (but more frequently without) the ornament of columns; around three sides of this hall are doors communicating with several bedchambers (among which is the porter's), the best of these being usually appropriated to country visitors. At the extremity of the hall, on either side to the right and left, if the house is large, there are two small recesses, rather than chambers, generally devoted to the ladies of the mansion; and in the centre of the tessellated pavement of the hall is invariably a square, shallow reservoir for rain water (classically termed impluvium), which was admitted by an aperture in the roof above; the said aperture being covered at will by an awning. Near this impluvium, which had a peculiar sanctity in the eyes of the ancients, were sometimes (but at Pompeii more rarely than at Rome) placed images of the household gods—the hospitable hearth, often mentioned by the Roman poets, and consecrated to the Lares, was at Pompeii almost invariably formed by a movable brazier; while in some corner, often the most ostentatious place, was deposited a huge wooden chest, ornamented and strengthened by bands of bronze or iron, and secured by strong hooks upon a stone pedestal so firmly as to defy the attempts of any robber to detach it from its position. It is supposed that this chest was the money-box, or coffer, of the master of the house; though as no money has been found in any of the chests discovered at Pompeii, it is probable that it was sometimes rather designed for ornament than use.

—Edward Bulwer-Lytton,
The Last Days of Pompeii (1842)

And then there's the ever-wretched Harry Stephen Keeler, who overwhelms the reader with detail about people who you might meet later (but probably won't, unless you have the stomach to continue reading the novel):

For it must be remembered that at the time I knew quite nothing, naturally, concerning Milo Payne, the mysterious Cockney-talking Englishman with the checkered long-beaked Sherlockholmsian cap; nor of the latter's "Barr-Bag" which was as like my own bag

as one Milwaukee wienerwurst is like another; nor of
Legga, the Human Spider, with her four legs and her
six arms; nor of Ichabod Chang, ex-convict, and son
of Dong Chang; nor of the elusive poetess, Abigail
Sprigge; nor of the Great Simon, with his 2163 pearl
buttons; nor of—in short, I then knew quite nothing
about anything or anybody involved in the affair of
which I had now become a part, unless perchance it
were my Nemesis, Sophie Kratzenschneiderwümpel—
or Suing Sophie!

—Harry Stephen Keeler,
Riddle of the Traveling Skull (1934)

◇◇◇◇◇

dialect, dreadful: Let us pause here and thank the literary
gods that few writers nowadays use execrable dialects in their
works. The idea of using dialect is laudable—it's intended to make
a character more realistic—but just try reading most of the stuff.
You'll find yourself nauseated, bored, irritated, and sometimes
offended.

Fake African American Dialect

"S'pose we must be resigned; but oh Lord! how ken I?
If I know'd anything whar you's goin', or how they'd
sarve you! Missis says she'll try and 'deem ye, in a
year or two; but Lor! nobody never comes up that

goes down thar! They kills 'em! I've hearn 'em tell how dey works 'em up on dem ar plantations."

—Harriet Beecher Stowe,
Uncle Tom's Cabin (1852)

◇

"Yassuh, A spose we caint keep dese ressavations."

—Ian Fleming, *Live and Let Die* (1954)

Fake Chinese Dialect

"You owe flowty dollee—me washee you camp."

—Bret Harte,
"The Latest Chinese Outrage" (1870)

◇

"Gleetings, Mistel Palladine," he called, smiling blandly across the room. "I maker big mis-took las' ni'te, w'en I sellee you sholt shoestlings, 'stead of long shoestling like you wan'. But I no likee bothel you this molnin' fo' to le' me extsange—you plob'ly lots busy in molnin's, yes, no?—but allee lite!—comee I now, aftel you' lunch, to makee extsange."

—Harry Stephen Keeler,
The Case of the 16 Beans (1944)

Fake Native American Dialect

Hoss thief and renegade pale-face. Don't like-im.
They make-im bad bargain with me just now . . .
Hy-yu-skookum!

—Kim Knight, *Nighthawk's Gold* (1939)

◇

Come catchum smoke. Cheterfiiel ceegret. Come back
byeumbye afta braves makum powow wit' Lomitaha.

—James O'Hanlon, *Murder at Horsethief* (1941)

Fake Mexican Dialect

"Muzzles for renegade dogs!" the little Mexican
screeched gleefully. "Come get thee lead muzzles,
sons of thee coyotes!"

—Ed Earl Repp, *Gun Hawk* (1937)

Fake Scottish Dialect

The bonnie Scotchman niver doot
   Wi' Scots Wauhai!
  That Santa Claus goes a' aboot . . .

—Fred Emerson Brooks,
"Foreigners on Santa Claus" (1890s)

Fake French Dialect

We Have ze Santa Claus een France
We see him when we get ze chance.
— Fred Emerson Brooks,
"Foreigners on Santa Claus" (1890s)

Fake British Dialect

"Your honour, forgive an eccentric old knight his foolish prejudice for the British court system. I realize I should have called the French authorities, but I'm a snob and I do not trust those laissez-faire French to prosecute properly. This man almost murdered me. Yes, I made a rash decision forcing my manservant to help me bring him to England, but I was under great stress. Mea culpa. Mea culpa."
— Dan Brown, *The Da Vinci Code* (2003)

Fake Arabic Dialect

This dancing woman upon the stage wears nothing but the hat of cowboys . . . This David Lee Roth, if there was time Bassam would find him and kill him.
— Andre Dubus III,
The Garden of Last Days (2008)

◇◇◇◇◇

dialogue, deadly: The essence of writing good dialogue is to sound natural and realistic—as if two people, i.e., humans, are actually *talking*. As with the following *completely* naturalistic excerpt:

> "Home again, mother?" he boldly uttered, as he gazed reverently in her face.
>
> "Home to Hades!" returned the raging high-bred daughter of distinguished effeminacy.
>
> "Ah me! what is the matter?" meekly inquired his lordship.
>
> "Everything is the matter with a broken-hearted mother of low-minded offspring," she answered hotly . . . "Henry Edward Ludlow Gifford, son of my strength, idolized remnant of my inert husband, who at this moment invisibly offers the scourging whip of fatherly authority to your backbone of resentment (though for years you think him dead to your movements) and pillar of maternal trust . . ."
>
> —Amanda McKittrick Ros, *Delina Delaney* (1898)

Ha ha! Yes, you have caught on to our clever ruse! This is terrible dialogue and we defy you to find anyone who actually speaks like this. And so the critics said, back in 1897 when this was published. But do not think wretched dialogue is restricted to the past. Here is some modern deadly dialogue just as stilted as that from the past.

"For you and I are both aware you need to get to know the 'me,' inside as well as out. Only then will you be able to capture my true essence. Every artist longs to capture his subject's true essence. The ability to do so is what separates the good from the truly great."

—Kathleen Lawless, *Taboo* (2003)

On the other hand, sometimes perfectly naturalistic dialogue is pretty deadly as well. Much like sitting on a train and overhearing the particularly painful conversation in front of you, complete with half sentences, abrupt stops, run-on sentences, banalities, and trivialities, reading this sort of overly naturalistic dialogue makes the reader yearn for an emergency brake.

"You don't have a neck."
"What?" . . .
"I have a neck."
"You do not."
"I do."
"You do not."
"I do."
"Where?"
"Where everyone has one."
"Point to it . . . I still don't see it. Make it come out."
"There."
"Where?"

—Walter Koenig,
Buck Alice and the Actor-Robot (1988)

It seems that dialogue should be natural sounding, then, but not too natural. Naturally.

◇◇◇◇◇

dialogue, deadly unromantic: A particularly peculiar subset of deadly dialogue is ostensibly romantic but decidedly unromantic dialogue. In this case, the writer uses well-chosen (or ill-chosen, as the case may be) conversation to illume the characters' romantic feelings.

> Remole sobered. "I been having crazy dreams of late. You know I'm not much on she-stuff around a spread, don't you? Well, I been sort of day-dreamin' about you and me . . . riding circle with our own chuck wagon on my own private range."
>
> "My Gawd, big boy, go on! I'm fair to droolin' at the mouth."
>
> —William Edmunds Claussen,
> *Rustlers of Slabrock* (1946)

◇

> "Pardon me, my friend," said he; "it cost me four years in a foreign land to travel to the frigid zone of my heart, where the snows that ended the summer of love were lighted only by the flitting meteors of the borealis race. But your unexpected presence here to-day, which I could not avoid, has placed that icy region again under the burning sun of the tropics. Already

the snows have gone, and their place is occupied by the water lily, perfumed with the spices and the cloves and spreading its sweet petals upon my bosom. How can you drive such love as mine from its mortal habitation and leave my bosom empty with all but wondering pain? My heart is thirsty, and you are its living fountain. Let me drink and water a desert that will soon flourish with the green bay-tree and the balm of Gilead."

"O God," she cried, "pardon the weakness of woman," and burying her face in his bosom, her lachrymal lakes overflowed and anointed his garments with drops that were to him the myrrh of the soul.

—Shepherd M. Dugger,
The Balsam Groves of the
Grandfather Mountain (1892)

It's enough to make your lachrymal lakes overflow, is it not?

◇◇◇◇◇

double entendres, unintended: Double entendres are phrases that mean something other than the obvious, something that (usually) is a tad risqué. Often a writer deliberately uses this in a tongue-in-cheek way. But we are more interested in those other times . . . the times when the double entendre is delightfully and happily unintended—allowing the reader a chuckle at the author's expense.

As you will see, this is especially common in older books since word meanings and slang have changed. So in most cases, the laughable double entendre was not the writer's fault but ours—for having minds which have learned modern usages and word changes—and which are perhaps a bit more open to salacious ideas.

And now, without further ado, some of our favorite unintended but delicious double entendres:

> She gave a little scream and a jerk, and so relieved herself.
>
> —Anthony Trollope, *The Duke's Children* (1879)

◇

> Then she had had her equal consciousness that, within five minutes, something between them had well, she couldn't call it anything but come.
>
> —Henry James, *The Wings of the Dove* (1902)

◇

> Mr. Grant, really glad of an excuse to dismount, offered his cock to Lydia, who immediately flung a leg over it . . .
>
> —Angela Thirkell, *The Brandons* (1953)

◇

> The only thing I can think about now is being hard up. I suppose having my hands in my pockets has made me think of this.
>
> —Jerome K. Jerome, *Idle Thoughts of an Idle Fellow* (1889)

The chief purpose of Mrs. Roosevelt in coming to London was to have intercourse with the American troops.

—Gilbert Harding, *Along My Line* (1953)

◇◇◇◇◇

dullness, literary: The wretched writer has the knack for taking an exciting idea and making it stultifyingly dull. This typically is accomplished by deftly removing the sense of immediacy from the novel and replacing it with, well, dullness.

For example, *Pamela* is the romantic story of a beautiful fifteen-year-old maid whose master starts making sexual advances at her. Sound exciting? It is not—chiefly because said sexual advances are only a few lines, while long-winded exposition in the form of letters home are many lines. Many, many, many lines. Boring ones. Read on . . .

> Well, I will now proceed with my sad story. And so, after I had dried my eyes, I went in, and began to ruminate with myself what I had best to do. Sometimes I thought I would leave the house and go to the next town, and wait an opportunity to get to you; but then I was at a loss to resolve whether to take away the things he had given me or no, and how to take them away: Sometimes I thought to leave them behind me, and only go with the clothes on my back, but then I

had two miles and a half, and a byway, to the town; and being pretty well dressed, I might come to some harm, almost as bad as what I would run away from; and then may-be, thought I, it will be reported, I have stolen something, and so was forced to run away; and to carry a bad name back with me to my dear parents, would be a sad thing indeed!—O how I wished for my grey russet again, and my poor honest dress, with which you fitted me out (and hard enough too it was for you to do it!) for going to this place, when I was not twelve years old, in my good lady's days! Sometimes I thought of telling Mrs. Jervis, and taking her advice, and only feared his command to be secret; for, thought I, he may be ashamed of his actions, and never attempt the like again: And as poor Mrs. Jervis depended upon him, through misfortunes, that had attended her, I thought it would be a sad thing to bring his displeasure upon her for my sake.

—Samuel Richardson, *Pamela* (1740)

The author in the above passage—by the clever use of complicated syntax, excess description of virtue, and long, drawn-out passages—created a masterpiece of boredom, at least for modern readers. Yet it was a bestseller in its time and, perhaps fittingly, was rendered into numerous lengthy sermons by admiring preachers of the Church of England. (Our guess is that the sermons were probably just as dull.)

And if you're still with us . . . let us bore you once more: Here, the novelist manages the virtually impossible—making a murder by strangling mind-numbingly dull. How does he accomplish this masterful feat? Endless detail, extraneous information, and long confusing sentences, of course. But here he adds a clever twist—he makes certain that the only possibly interesting thing—i.e., the murder—happens offscreen! The result is deadlier than the murder itself.

> The discovery was made in a search of his private papers, and consisted of an old yellow newspaper clipping . . . Inspector Allan Jamison, a typographical expert at Scotland Yard, identified the type as being London Times type of 1910 . . . As for the item itself, it occupied but a few hundred words, and lay in a most obscure position in the column, being sandwiched between the annual letter from the enthusiastic reader who sees the first robin of the season in St. James Park, and the customary letter advocating the return to England of the good old Tory Party . . . The significant thing about Marceau's letter, however, in view of the rationale of his own murder, was that in its last line it modestly set forth that the most painless form of legal euthanasia, for such small people, would be strangling . . . Such—the only ascertainable illumination as to the motive for the bizarre murder of André Marceau: insane resentment on the part of a single member of a group of curious people—the heterogeneous world of Lilliputia—flaring into existence after 25 long years—a group which comprises members of every race and blood, which numbers among itself hundreds of new recruits gained by births since that

letter was written—insane resentment against a man who, himself generously endowed with size by Nature, had urged their extinguishment from the scheme of things—by the most painful of all deaths—strangling!
—Harry Stephen Keeler, *The Marceau Case* (1936)

◇◇◇◇◇

eumerdification: This term, coined by philosopher Daniel Dennet after a conversation with Michel Foucault, means "Making academic writing at least 25% incomprehensible crap, to seem smarter." Academic writers are eumerdifying wretched writers par excellence. They generate enormous amounts of verbal (and adjectival, nounal, and pronounal) crap every year and probably contribute considerably to the warming of the planet.

A brief ("brief" being a relative term here) glance at most academic writing will bear this out. Typically, the point (if there is one) or subject (ditto) is buried under a great heaping mound of words that emits such a stench that one is overcome by the fumes and misses said point or subject.

To wit:

The lure of imaginary totality is momentarily frozen before the dialectic of desire hastens on within symbolic chains.

—Fred Botting,
Making Monstrous: Frankenstein,
Criticism, Theory (1991)

Since thought is seen to be "rhizomatic" rather than "arboreal," the movement of differentiation and becoming is already imbued with its own positive trajectory.
—Richard Kearney and Mara Rainwater, eds.,
The Continental Philosophy Reader (1996)

[Ed. note: This won an award from the Bad Writing Contest in 1996; it retains its pungency even today, rhizomatically speaking. Or is it arboreally speaking? We are confused.]

In Chapters 4 and 5, I return to the foreskin, the fantasized remnant of the Christian typological imaginary, in order to question the Lacanian argument that there can be no "pre-modern" uncanny. What supercessionary fantasies are at stake in the Lacanian claim that the uncanny is only constitutive of the modern? I argue that these Lacanian arguments mistake the uncanny for the foreskin.

They cannot think that within the phallus there lodges the temporal kernal of the circumsized foreskin, of the temporality which is not one. I argue that the foreskin is the "unhistorical" (not ahistorical) remainder of the uncanny that is the unassimilable temporality that exceeds their Lacanian periodization of the uncanny.
—Kathleen Biddick,
*The Typological Imaginary:
Circumcision, Technology, History* (2003)

[Ed. note: We know she is talking about penises. Actually, we think she is talking about penises. But beyond that, we are not sure.]

As my story is an august tale of fathers and sons, real and imagined, the biography here will fitfully attend to the putative traces in Manet's work of "les noms du père," a Lacanian romance of the errant paternal phallus ("Les Non-dupes errent"), a revised Freudian novella of the inferential dynamic of paternity which annihilates (and hence enculturates) through the deferred introduction of the third term of insemination the phenomenologically irreducible dyad of the mother and child.

—Steven Z. Levine,
in *Twelve Views of Manet's "Bar"* (1996)

◇

Punctuated by what became ubiquitous sound bites—Tonya dashing after the tow truck, Nancy sailing the ice with one leg reaching for heaven—this melodrama parsed the transgressive hybridity of un-narrativized representative bodies back into recognizable hetero-visual codes.

—Robyn Wiegman and Lynda Zwinger,
"Tonya's Bad Boot," in *Women on Ice*,
ed. Cynthia Baughman (1995)

◇

This is the real exteriority of the absolute outside: the reality of the absolutely unconditioned absolute outside univocally predicated of the dark: the light univocally predicated of the darkness: the shining of the light univocally predicated of the limit of the darkness: actuality univocally predicated of the other of self-identity: existence univocally predicated of the absolutely unconditioned other of the self. The precision of the shining of the light breaking the dark is the other-identity of the light. The precision of the absolutely minimum transcendence of the dark is the light itself/the absolutely unconditioned exteriority of existence for the first time/the absolutely facial identity of existence/the proportion of the new creation *sans* depth/the light itself *ex nihilo*: the dark itself univocally identified, i.e., not self-identity identity itself equivocally, not the dark itself equivocally, in "self-alienation," not "self-identity, itself in self-alienation" "released" in and by "otherness," and "actual other," "itself," not the abysmal inversion of the light, the reality of the darkness equivocally, absolute identity equivocally predicated of the self/selfhood equivocally predicated of the dark (the reality of this darkness the other-self-covering of identity which is the identification person-self).

—D. G. Leahy,
Foundation: Matter the Body Itself (1996)

[Ed. note: This, to us, and presumably to the University of Nebraska Press editor who first alerted the world to this selection, appears closer to 100% than 25% merde . . . unequivocally.]

exceptions, exceptionally execrable: Some wretched writers fall into an exceptional trap. Literally. They begin describing something, then seem to change their mind, so they counteract the initial description with a handy "except for." It winds up sounding as though the writer realized his or her mistake, but was too lazy to backspace and delete.

> It looked entirely normal, except that the sheath was made entirely of lead, and it covered the sword entirely.
>
> —Brent Weeks, *The Way of Shadows* (2008)

◇

> There was silence for a few minutes. Silence, that is, except for the whining noise, which continued to grow.
>
> —Bron Fane (Lionel Fanthorpe),
> *The Intruders* (1962)

This type of wretched writing is execrable . . . except when it isn't.

◇◇◇◇◇

eyes, roving: As with other body parts (see page 20), eyes are extremely active in wretched writing. In fact, they are so active that they merit a closer look, so to speak . . .

Most often, eyes are (apparently) plucked from the skull and tossed about willy-nilly.

> She threw her eyes upon the walls, and saw their shattered condition.
>
> —Ann Radcliffe,
> *The Mysteries of Udolpho* (1794)

◇

> With a desperate effort I wrenched my eyes from the hypnotic glare of the snake. I rolled them toward the door. I dared move no further.
>
> —Elizabeth Peters,
> *Crocodile on the Sandbank* (2008)

◇

> Marjorie would often take her eyes from the deck and cast them far out to sea.
>
> —Ursula Bloom, *A Voyage of Discovery* (1964)

Eyes often do things of their own (often very athletic) volition. They scamper, they romp, they run!

> His eyes roamed around the workshop, knocking over tables and equipment, until they settled on my Master . . .
>
> —Matthew Skelton, *Endymion Spring* (2006)

◇

His eyes ran like weasels over the faces of the other players . . .

—Philip José Farmer, "Attitudes" (1953)

◇

Her jolly brown eyes made a complete circuit round my head . . .

—E. F. Benson, "Home, Sweet Home" (1928)

◇

She took a few paces within, her amber eyes clambering up library steps, sliding along polished shelves housing neatly ranged books within a mellow wood gallery then down the stairs on the opposite side of the room.

—Mary Brendan, *The Silver Squire* (2001)

◇

"Seigneur, I have invented forty new dishes for tonight's banquet," Francois said pathetically, his eyes creeping out until they hung on the rims of their sockets like desperate people wavering on the edges of precipices.

—George Viereck and Paul Eldridge,
Salome, the Wandering Jewess (1930)

It can be a bit unsettling to be beset with all of these eyes. So, in closing:

> Their hostess firmly put an end to the morbid discussion by collecting the ladies' eyes.
>
> —Nicholas Blake,
> *The Corpse in the Snowman* (1941)

◇◇◇◇◇

favorite words, overuse of: All of us have our favorite words or phrases. We are partial to the word "apoplectic" and the phrase "to tell the truth," for example. But while it is admirable to share these word or phrase partialities with one's readers, it is wretched to slobber such all over the pages. It gets messy. In fact, it makes us apoplectic, to tell the truth.

The works of techno-novelist Tom Clancy immediately spring to mind. Among various other annoyances, Mr. Clancy loves to use the word "lit" (instead of "turn on") when referring to computers. In his bestseller *Teeth of the Tiger*, turning a few pages, we find: "Jack lit up his computer." "He lit up his laptop." "After lighting up his computer," etc., etc. As one deeply anguished Amazon reviewer put it, "[I] prayed for a simple 'turned on' even 'fired up' but that was not to be." For us, too, instead of being turned on—or should we say "lit"—by this repetitious prose, we were turned off. Or lit off.

Lit off?

But another popular novelist, Dan Brown, is the world champion of favorite word overusage—particularly the overuse of the word and, indeed, the actual *concept*, of "lifting one's eyebrows." The man is absolutely fascinated by them. Eyebrows figure on virtually every other page of text in his book *Digital Fortress* (as noted by the excellent blog Language Log). (Well, not quite, but so frequently one wonders about weird proclivities and all sorts of things one shouldn't ponder of respectable writers.) Turning a few pages, we find:

> Page 13: "Susan arched her eyebrows coyly"
> Page 28: "Strathmore arched his eyebrows"
> Page 54: "Strathmore raised his eyebrows"
> Page 55: "Strathmore raised an eyebrow"
> Page 76: "Strathmore raised his eyebrows expectantly"
> Page 104: "Hale arched a surprised eyebrow"
> Page 140: "Raising her eyebrows in mock anticipation"
> Page 141: "Rocío raised her eyebrows"
> Page 148: "Rocío arched her eyebrows"
> Page 186: "Brinkerhoff arched his eyebrows"
> Page 253: "Numataka arched his eyebrows"
> Page 369: "The enormous man arched his eyebrows"
> Page 396: "Smith arched his eyebrows, impressed"
> Page 408: "He arched his eyebrows, obviously impressed"

Guess what *our* eyebrows are doing right now?

flowery language, inappropriate: For some reason, some wretched writers feel compelled to take a rather disgusting subject and spray the literary equivalent of air freshener on it. Take the following, an article written back in 1892:

> And on the field of battle which preventive medicine is now and everywhere waging against the ills to which flesh is heir, the banner of preventive constipation is well at the front. Indeed I feel confident and I do greatly rejoice in this assurance, that when the enthusiastic physician who is ever loyal to the guild, who keeps her escutcheon fair and stainless, who is ever jealous of her honor, shall proudly make mention of her achievements and will not then be omitted.
>
> —*American Practitioner and News*
> (August 13, 1892)

Keep in mind, this writer is discussing constipation. All the flowery words in the world won't change that, no matter what he may think. Similarly, the following is still just about pee.

> Male urination really is a kind of accomplishment, an arc of transcendence . . . Male urination is a form of commentary . . . A male dog marking every bush on the block is a graffiti artist, leaving his rude signature with each lift of the leg.
>
> —Camille Paglia, *Sexual Personae* (1990)

food imagery, bad: We all eat; thus we all can relate to food. It is this universality that makes allusion to food such a common literary device. But in the wrong hands, food imagery can be—well, let's just say a recipe for disaster. Let's take a look at some of the specific ingredients that make a nauseating stew

Chocolate

He smiles down at her nipple, which is brown as a bar of Belgian chocolate, aureole the size of a round of individual cheese and nipple itself a surprisingly chunky square of crinkled flesh.
—Cory Doctorow, *Eastern Standard Tribe* (2004)

Pancakes

Three little wrinkles like a stack of tiny pancakes sit just at the top of Nicolas Cage's nose, held in place by his bushy, Italian-guy eyebrows, which extend out and down like two hairy arms around his for-the-moment strangely vacant blue eyes.
—Larissa MacFarquhar,
"Stranger in Paradise," interview with Nicolas Cage, *Premiere Magazine* (June 1997)

Chili

And then he was fully socketed to her, like a pipe wrench in a crock of warm chili.
—Robert Tanenbaum, *Act of Revenge* (2000)

[Ed. note: Why is there a pipe wrench in a crock of chili? Wouldn't a spoon—a thick spoon, if the author wants to make a point—make more sense?]

Lemons

She squeezed her thighs together as if trying to juice a lemon.
—Jaid Black, *Hunter's Oath* (2006)

Twinkies

He could feel the dampness between her legs just from where they pressed together like Twinkies inside their cellophane wrapper.
—Heidi Betts, *A Bite Before Christmas* (2011)

[Ed. note: Thank God the Twinkies are still in their wrapper.]

Roasted Turkey (Basted)

Despite being tight, his jeans fell away like butter sliding off a roasting turkey, and his erection spilled out, swollen and wanting.

—Lynsay Sands,
Hungry for You: An Argeneau Novel (2010)

An Entire Produce Department

Sandy-blonde hair to her shoulders, held up in a simple ponytail by a green rubber band fresh off the newspaper. No makeup. Strong back, long lines. Rigid and stern, but also graceful. Cold but quietly beautiful. Complicated and busy, but also in need. More like an onion than a banana. Her eyes looked like the green that sits just beneath the peel of an avocado, and her lips like the red part of the peach that sits up next to the seed.

—Charles Martin, *When Crickets Cry* (2006)

foreshadowing, bludgeoning: Foreshadowing done deftly can enhance the texture of a book. It's a way for the writer to drop a hint to the readers, a nuance of what is to come. Even if readers don't pick up on it, the foreshadowing adds to the mood and depth of the writing. But foreshadowing done wretchedly is the equivalent of a neon sign flashing at the reader. An ugly, annoying neon sign, at that. One that the writer is using as a bludgeon to whack the reader on the head. Hard.

> On the way back they passed a billboard advertising an airline. In the warm glow of happiness that enveloped her, the caption on the billboard did not strike her as even faintly ominous. It said, "Fly Now—Pay Later."
> —Jeanne Hines, *Bride of Terror* (1976)

> GIRL: Excuse me—how far is it to Camp Crystal Lake?
> [Everyone looks at her in horror]
> WAITRESS: [After an ominous silence] What is it, Enis, about twenty miles?
> TRUCK DRIVER: About that.
> LOCAL WOMAN: Camp *Blood*? They're opening that place again?
> —Script from *Friday the 13th* (1980)

[Ed. note: Gee, you don't think anything bad will happen at Camp Crystal Lake, do you? Not to give anything away, but we kinda think there's trouble ahead . . .]

◇◇◇◇◇

funny-sounding names, excessive use of: The astute writer must choose his or her character and place-names very carefully—and use such chosen names *judiciously*. Two rather simple rules of thumb to follow: (1) Don't use too many weird-sounding and hard-to-follow names, and (2) Especially don't use too many weird-sounding and hard-to-follow names *all in a row*.

Following these rules is all the more important when writing a historical, fantasy, or science fiction novel. On one hand, the writer must strive for verisimilitude—who wants, for example, to read about an ancient Greek character named Bob or a cave-woman named Tiffany? On the other hand . . .

> "But tell me this also farmer," Epaminondas pressed even closer, still grinning at upping the Thespian. "Think when you have wasps with the sharp tails in your vineyard that Malgis planted. You know the terrible black ones. The ones that sting the paws of sleeping Sturax over there. Or land on the nose of Porpax. Or even in their pride jab the tall legs of your Neto or the chest of buxom Damo—do you chase them all over the orchard, flailing at one or two of them with the broom or clapping at them with your hands?"
>
> "Of course, not!" Odd that the Theban knew of Neto and his son's wife Damo, and of Chion and apparently Sturax and Porpax too, but at least not Gorgos as well.
>
> —Victor Davis Hanson, *The End of Sparta* (2011)

◇

> I am Ayla of the Ninth Cave of the Zeladonii, acolyte of the Zeladonii, First Among Those Who Serve The

Great Earth Mother, mated to Jondalar, Master Flint-Knapper and brother of Joharran, leader of the Ninth Cave of the Zeladonii. I was Daughter of the Mammoth Hearth of the Lion Camp of the Mamutoi, Chosen to be the spirit of the Cave Lion, Protected by the Cave Bear, and friend of the horses Whinney, Racer, and Gray, and the four-legged hunter, Wolf.

—Jean M. Auel,
The Land of Painted Caves (2011)

◇

They told me of the Yagas . . . in the grim city of Yugga, on the rock Yuthla, by the river Yogh, in the land of Yagg . . . Their ruler was a black queen named Gasmen.

—Robert E. Howard, *Almuric* (1939)

[Ed. note: Is Yaga in Yagg or Yagg in Yogh or Yagas?]

Yes, a barrage of ostensibly versimilitudinous names can wind up being, as Epaminondas or Neto or Sturax or Porpax might have said in their native Greek tongue, "kaka."

◇◇◇◇◇

genitalia, romantic euphemisms for: Novelist Terry Pratchett once wrote: "Mind you, the Elizabethans had so many words for the female genitals that it is quite hard to speak a sentence of modern English without inadvertently mentioning at least three of them."

Prachett could just as well be talking about wretched writers, particularly wretched romance writers. They aggressively and enthusiastically use euphemisms for the male and female genitals in an active effort to avoid sounding excessively clinical. A laudable idea indeed. But the problem is the words they use instead—and the fact that they use the same euphemisms over and over and over. And over.

We begin with women. More specifically, with clitorises. Or as wretched writers often call them, buttons. In reading different romance novels, we ran across private buttons, womanly buttons and feminine buttons, secret buttons, pulsing buttons, exploding buttons (our personal favorite), warm buttons, fiery buttons, and similarly, buttons of heat.

And speaking of "buttons of heat," vaginas, too, are usually quite hot. And we mean this in the literal sense . . .

> The hot pool in her woman place turned scalding with heat, and that secret spot she'd newly discovered under the feather's duress seemed to swell and throb.
> —Sandra Hill, *The Bewitched Viking* (1998)

You'll note that Ms. Hill has successfully incorporated three romantic tropes in the one sentence: the hot pool, the secret spot, and the swelling and throbbing. This trio is very popular where vaginal tissue is concerned. Add a fourth—moistness in some form or other—and you have the quintessential quiff, if you will.

> Queer tingles raced from the stiff little peak in all directions. Deep in the soft, secret place between her thighs

Storm felt a slow, burning ache flicker, take flame, and begin to blaze like wildfire through her loins.

—Rebecca Brandewyne, *Love, Cherish Me* (1983)

◇

the most intimate, begging part of her . . .
the moist folds that seeped with desire.

—Vivian Vaughan, *Sunrise Surrender* (1993)

◇

Pink, weeping flesh, the tiny kernel of flesh hidden in her cleft.

—Samantha James, *Every Wish Fulfilled* (1997)

◇

The weeping furnace of her sheath.

—Stephanie Laurens, *The Brazen Bride* (2010)

There is a good reason vaginas are so often called sheaths. What is sheathed in a sheath? Yes, you're right . . . a man's "throbbing sword." Or his sword of (yes) fire, manly sword, masculine sword, or straining sword. And in some cases, the hero is so well endowed a mere sword doesn't cut it . . .

Christian's manroot jumped against her thigh and she imagined it a velvet-tipped iron spear. He would render her vulnerable, she would yield, then he would conquer her with his formidable weapon!

—Virginia Henley, *Desired* (2009)

Of course, sometimes writers eschew the typical sword/spear/weapon penile euphemism and opt for something a tad more unique . . .

> "Is that your tallywhacker?"
>> —Jackie Weger, *Eye of the Beholder* (1987)

◇◇◇◇◇

genitalia, unintended literary sightings of: The prudent writer must be ever on the alert for hidden testicles, phalli, vaginae, and the like. These body parts have an unfortunate tendency to insert themselves in one's prose when least expected. This happens even to the best writers—who have their occasional wretched moments.

> Such was Catherine Morland at ten. At fifteen appearances were mending; she began to curl her hair and long for balls.
>> —Jane Austen, *Northanger Abbey* (1818)

◇

> "You're overtasked, good Simon Lee, Give me your tool," to him I said.
>> —William Wordsworth,
>> "Simon Lee, the Old Huntsman" (1798)

Next after that slow-coming, slow-going smile of her lover, it was the rusty complexion of his patrimonial marbles that she most prized.

—Henry James, "The Last of the Valerii" (1885)

◇

He, as he told his tale, did not look her in the face, but sat with his eyes fixed upon her muff.

—Anthony Trollope,
The Last Chronicle of Barset (1867)

◇

"If you have Miss Moffat," said Alexandrina, "you must have dear little pussy, too; and I really think that pussy is too young."

—Anthony Trollope, *Doctor Thorne* (1858)

◇

Pussy, Jack, and many of 'em! . . .
And now, Jack, let's have a little talk about Pussy. Two pairs of nutcrackers?

—Charles Dickens,
The Mystery of Edwin Drood (1870)

Genitalia allusions can be a problem when titling a book as well, even a scholarly or highly technical work, like, say, an engineering book about, er, structures that perform well and are, um, stiff. The following title comes to mind:

Designing High Performance Stiffened Structures, by Imeche (Institution of Mechanical Engineers)

◇◇◇◇◇

hipster writing, embarrassingly unhip: For some reason, some writers feel a need to sound "cool," "with it," even—dare we say—"hep." This is most embarrassing to the reader. It is horribly reminiscent of well-meaning adults trying to talk like teenagers.

Take, for example, these lines of highly hip dialogue by Tom Clancy (please) from *The Teeth of the Tiger* . . . which will set your own teeth on edge:

> "Who's wog number two, I wonder," Brian said. "I don't know, and we can't freelance. You packin'?" Dominic asked. "Bet your bippy, bro. You?" "Hang a big roger on that," Dominic answered.
> —Tom Clancy, *The Teeth of the Tiger* (2003)

Bet your bippy? Oh, bro, what have you wrought . . .

Sometimes the ostensibly hip writer is more like a high school nerd with a pocket protector trying (and failing) to sound like the cool kids. This seems to be the case with columnist David Brooks:

> She still thought it was a sign of social bravery to be a crude-talking, hard-partying, cotton candy lipstick-wearing, thong-snapping, balls-to-the-wall disciple in the church of Lady GaGa.

With his friends he was all "Yo! Douche bag!" but in parental and polite adult company he used a language and set of mannerisms based on the pretence that he'd never gone through puberty.

   —David Brooks, *The Social Animal* (2011)

◇

America is creative because of its moral materialism—when social values and economic ambitions get down in the mosh pit and dance.

   —David Brooks, "A New Social Agenda,"
   The New York Times (2012)

Writers can fall into the embarrassing fake hip trap even when they're postulating the cool lingo of the future:

"Back in the twentieth century," he explained, "Bellman of the Rand Corporation predicted 2% of the work force would be able to produce all the country could consume by the year 2000 and . . ." "Don't roach me funker," she said. "And don't shirk off in your electro-steamer. This mopsy wants to poke."

   —Mack Reynolds, *Commune 2000 A.D.* (1974)

This kind of writing makes *these* mopsies want to puke.

◇◇◇◇◇

hipster writing, horribly outdated: There is another category of hipster writing that winds up being rotten not necessarily because of the writing itself, but because of its timeliness or lack thereof. The cool factor is lost in the past . . . and the hip words wind up sounding ridiculous.

This is particularly true of screenwriting:

> Christy, what is this jazz you puttin' down about our planet being round? Everybody hip that it's square!
>
> —John Drew Barrymore,
> paraphrasing what Queen Isabella
> said to Columbus,
> *High School Confidential* (1958)

> GIRL: "Don't look at me like that. I can read your head. Dolly and Patty have nothing to do with thee and me."
>
> GUY: "I don't . . . I don't wanna hear any more about them dykes. And if you don't cool this lickety-split-talk-talk jazz, you're gonna get my paranoid goin' too, ya dig?"
>
> —Beatnik girl and boyfriend
> discussing two lesbians at another table,
> in *Once a Thief* (1965)

◇

"You know what I want to be? Nothing, you dig? If you can't dig "nothing," you can't dig anything. Dig?"
—John Phillip Law as a hippie in *Skidoo* (1968)

Yes. We dig.

◇◇◇◇◇

historical dialogue, hysterical: Historical dialogue occupies an interesting double slot in the annals of wretched writing, both in novels and films, as writers typically fall into two schools.

First, the wretched old-fashioned method—in which people seem to have sticks up their ass and speak in very rigid formalities, complete with peculiar yet perfect sentence structure.

"Abjure this woman and her idolatries. Tear down the obscene abomination she has erected!"
—*Solomon and Sheba* (1959)

◇

"And what," said his low, deep voice, "brings thee, O maiden! to the house of the Eastern stranger?"

"His fame," replied Julia.

"In what?" said he, with a strange and slight smile.

"Canst thou ask, O wise Arbaces? Is not thy knowledge the very gossip theme of Pompeii?"

"Some little lore have I indeed, treasured up," replied Arbaces: "but in what can such serious and
sterile secrets benefit the ear of beauty?"

—Edward Bulwer-Lytton,
The Last Days of Pompeii (1834)

[Ed. note: Ear of beauty?]

GENGHIS KHAN: I shall keep you, Bortai. I shall keep
you unresponding to my passion. Your hatred
will kindle into love.
BORTAI: Before that day dawns, Mongol, the vultures
will feast on your heart!

—*The Conqueror* (1956)

Then there's the wretched modern method—in which people
might look like they're from the past, but other than that, you
could run into them at the mall . . .

"It's not just about how far we've come, it's this bitch
of a wind."

—*Christopher Columbus: The Discovery* (1992)

◇

"Michelangelo, make up your mind, once and for all:
do you want to finish that ceiling?"

—*The Agony and the Ecstasy* (1965)

Last, but certainly not least, there is plain old vanilla bad historical writing.

Eliza said, "Your father really thinks it's dangerous for us to remain here? It's ever so peaceful. I love the river, my garden, the wild deer that visit. I love all the wildlife except the alligators that sleep on our bank. I saw a huge fellow sunning himself this morning. When I was nine, one ate my favorite cat . . . "

—John Jakes, *Charleston* (2003)

◇

"War! War! That's all you think of, Dick Plantagenet! You burner! You pillager!"

—*King Richard and the Crusaders* (1954)

homophonilia, horrific: Homophoniliacs are a subset of wretched writers who often love proving their supposed erudition—by misusing homophones to the detriment of good writing. Homophones are, as we're sure you know, words that sound the same but are spelled differently. However, herein lies the rub: *There meanings are usually different.* The not-terribly-alert reader will note that we have just used a homophone incorrectly. Now, humbly, we will correct ourselves: *Their* meanings are usually different.

Homophoniliacs are usually blithely unaware of such incorrect usages and use them either through ignorance or, more commonly, a desire to sound intellectual. For some reason, homophoniliacs often get it into their thick heads that homophones sound more "intellectual" than the dull normal word, as in these "discreet" versus (or should we say verses?) "discrete" homophone examples.

> Hottest Adult Toys Shipped Discretely To Your Door . . .
> so nobody but you will know what was ordered.
>
> —Craigslist ad

◇

> Buy Viagra safely and discretely at our Viagra pharmacy.
>
> —Spam email

If you're buying adult toys, you'd probably want them shipped discreetly—in plain brown wrappers—to your door rather than shipped to you one at a time, with clear labeling announcing to the world your latest vibrator. Ditto for Viagra. We assume the writer did not mean to infer that one could buy Viagra on a pill-by-pill basis. But clearly these writers got caught in an Intellectual Homophonilia trap.

There also is careless homophonilia, as in this *New York Times* film review.

> [The star] finds a room in a cheap hotel and picks up
> a job peddling a delivery bicycle for a butcher.
>
> —*The New York Times* (February 20, 1998)

[Ed. note: The star presumably does not sell a delivery bicycle for the butcher over and over, unless this is a very strange film.]

We'll admit that some of these errors might be due to overenthusiastic reliance on spell-check programs. We ourselves have run into this problem. But we expect that those who are paid to edit copy should find and hunt down these errors.

So let's reign in our overenthusiasm, yolk ourselves to a grammar book, and move foreword.

◇◇◇◇◇

imagery, aquatic fauna: We do not know why but it seems that certain writers like using fish, reptile, or aquatic fowl imagery in their works.

It is this that forces a reader to imagine semen as eel (or slime creature, if you will) . . .

> The suddenness of it, the snaking of her tongue, the pressure of her lips, the hot grip of her mouth, triggered his orgasm, which was not juice at all but a demon eel thrashing in his loins and swimming swiftly up his cock, one whole creature of live slime fighting the stiffness as it rose and bulged at the tip and darted into her mouth.
>
> —Paul Theroux, *Blinding Light* (2005)

And the semen-producing organ as a very active salmon (which is not only going home to spawn, but also, apparently, to very interestingly and very unusually for a penis, separate grain from a plant).

> The thing inside her jerked and threshed, a rising
> salmon, plunging home to spawn.
> > —Wendy Perriam,
> > *Dreams, Demons and Desire* (2001)

Here, the writer creatively uses piscine imagery to describe not a physical thing, but an emotion that is like a physical thing. (In fact, come to think of it, much like the very active salmon above.)

> Excitement leaped like a trout in the public trousers.
> > —Thomas Harris, *Hannibal* (1999)

Finally, we present another emotion—this one like an aquatic fowl. And fowl it is.

[Ed. note: Please forgive us for that.]

> Terror quacked like a choking duck in Dirk's chest,
> and he couldn't get his voice to work.
> > —A. A. Attanasio, *Arc of the Dream* (1986)

◇◇◇◇◇

imagery, too unique: It is good to be creative when painting a picture with your words, yes. However, sometimes a writer should think twice about the imagery he or she is using. "But," some writers seem to think, "this is an image, unlike any I have ever seen." Hmm. Perhaps there is a reason no other writer has come up with it, think we. Yet the intrepid excessively unique imagist presses on. Thus we the readers are blessed (or cursed, as the case may be) with examples like the following:

> The sirens and the noises of the crowd were loud through the thin walls, the broken skylight—through which a beam of light flashed, glaring yellow, stabbing like a finger on an ant.
>
> —Craig Thomas, *Playing with Cobras* (1993)

◇

> Sugar pretending to seduce an invisible man, begging him in a voice almost hysterical with lust. "Oh, you must let me stroke your balls, they are so beautiful—like . . . like a dog turd. A dog turd nestling under your . . ."
>
> —Michel Faber,
> *The Crimson Petal and the White* (2003)

◇

> They gathered pace as they walked. The passageway grew narrow and low, causing them to crouch as they stumbled on. The sound of water grew louder, and the gusting of the wind was like the eerie farting of a giant animal.
>
> —G. P. Taylor,
> *The Curse of Salamander Street* (2006)

imagery, uniquely inappropriate: While some writers fall into the trap of getting excessively unique with their imagery, others—in their zeal for creativity—wind up describing things in imagistic terms that are also unique, but also terribly, totally, and horribly inappropriate for the subject at hand.

For example, the concept of spaceships and the like being like a lacy bra and panties doesn't quite work. Nor does delving into a film role really remind us of the act of retching up a hair ball. And . . . there's worse!

> With listeners leaning over the velvet restraining ropes and angling for pictures, John Glenn urged them to re-member Shepard's 1961 Redstone flight in its political context, when the Soviet Union was seducing world opinion with the lingerie of Earth-orbiting technology.
> —Billy Cox, "Shepard Statue Honors
> American Space Cowboys,"
> *Florida Today* (March 24, 2000)

◇

> In "Private Confessions," Ullmann doesn't just direct one of the pivotal chapters of Bergman's childhood, she reaches deep into the distant heart of Bergman's crisp, artistic soul and untangles one gigantic hairball of feeling.
> —*Vancouver Sun* (reprinted in *The New Yorker,*
> January 2000)

If you read his [Jack London's] work today, you can see literary semen spraying across the American century.

—Columnist Johann Hari,
The Independent (August 23, 2010)

◇

Something more than a seducer-counselor is necessary to ease the excessive constipation of the region: What the Middle East needs now is a powerful purgative that will unblock the system and deliver the parties to the negotiating table.

—Douglas Davis,
The Australian (December 2, 2002)

◇◇◇◇◇

impossibilities: We must admire wretched writers for accomplishing the impossible in their writing. They boldly break the rules of logic, they cheerfully shatter the laws of physics, and even in science fiction, where some degree of weirdness is expected, they smoothly violate their own internal rules. Living in the wretched writer's universe is living in an impossible world that is somehow, strangely, wretchedly . . . *possible.*

Or should we say impossibly possible?

We do not know. We are confused.

Here are some charmingly contradictory impossibilities, everything from triangular circles to limited unlimited ranges.

> It was one of those perfect June nights that so seldom occur except in August.
> —Frankfort Moore, "Reggie's Rival" (1895)

[Ed. note: June nights, to the best of our knowledge, tend only to occur in June.]

> "Mmmmmm," said Maginty. It was an unwriteable, unpronounceable burble.
> —John E. Muller, *Dark Continuum* (1964)

[Ed. note: "Mmmmmm" seems both pretty writable and pronounceable to us.]

> Their range was, within limits, virtually unlimited.
> —A. J. Merak, *No Dawn and No Horizon* (1959)

[Ed note: Unlimited limits?]

> The dull-red mists seemed to flow together, enclosing the three sides of a circle.
> —Murray Leinster, *The Forgotten Planet* (1954)

[Ed. note: We are tempted to say circles have four sides, but we won't.]

The last chance to stop the operation had passed by.
The die was now cast, if not yet thrown.

—Tom Clancy, *Debt of Honor* (1994)

[Ed. note: Casting the die is throwing it, Tom.]

◇◇◇◇◇

jacket copy, bad: Here are two very simple concepts: (1) Jacket copy is the writing on the dust jacket of the book *[Ed. note: Or on the virtual dust jacket]*, and (2) Jacket copy is written to entice the browser into *buying* the book. Simple enough. But apparently some blurb writers haven't quite gotten the gist of Concept 2.

The result: bad jacket copy that is . . .

Boring and Obvious

This book is an attempt to show how, in the writer's view, the past has led to the present situation in world affairs.

—Lionel Curtis, *Civitas Dei*, Volume 2 (1938)

Confusing and Irritating

The universe has fallen into bloody chaos now that the dread empire of the tyrannical Shaa is no more at the mercy of the merciless Naxid who, freed from subjugation, now hunger for domination.

—Walter Jon Williams, *Conventions of War* (2005)

Confusing and Boring

Kester Weidmann, a half-crazed millionaire, believes that his dead brother's corpse can be reanimated by Voodoo, and contacts Rollo, crook night-club proprietor, who has negro employees. Rollo, seeing a fortune in the deal, plans to arrange a Voodoo seance. Kester's chauffeur, who is under a debt of gratitude to Kester, steals the body in order to prevent Rollo from obtaining it. Celie, Rollo's mistress, is also involved in the plot, and Susan Hedder is planted at Rollo's club by Kester's chauffeur to watch Kester. After many thrills there is a grand game of hunt-the-slipper with the corpse for the slipper. The magnificent finale is worthy of Hamlet and the excitement is maintained throughout.

—James Hadley Chase (Raymond Marshall),
Make the Corpse Walk (1946)

Excessively Creative

Just admit it. You've wondered what it would be like to have a boyfriend with wings and scales and a tail. You've wondered what it would be like to walk through the mall and have people move out of your way because they don't want to anger the dragon's wench.

—G. A. Aiken, *Dragon Actually* (2008)

Not Creative at All

Two and a half millennia ago, the artifact appeared in a remote corner of space, beside a trillion-year-old dying sun from a different universe. It was a perfect black-body sphere, and it did nothing. Then it disappeared.

Now it is back.

—Iain M. Banks, *Excession* (1996)

◇◇◇◇◇

legalese: Legalese is a very specific type of language written, as you'd expect, by lawyers—who typically make their money by billing their clients by the hour. Perhaps this is why they write things in such a verbose manner. It takes longer both to write *and* to read.

For example, let's see how the concept of "bigness" is described in legalese.

"Complex litigation" as used in these rules, includes one of more related cases which present unusual problems and which require extraordinary treatment, including but not limited to the cases ordinarily designated as "protracted" or "big."

—From the local rules of the U.S. District Court
in Seattle, Washington

And if you were ever unclear as to what *exactly* your buttocks are, let's let a lawyer explain:

Buttocks: The area at the rear of the human body (sometimes referred to as the glutaeus maximus) which lies between two imaginary lines running parallel to the ground when a person is standing, the first or top of such line being one-half inch below the top of the vertical cleavage of the nates (ie the prominence formed by the muscles running from the back of the hip to the back of the leg) and the second or bottom line being one-half inch above the lowest point of curvature of the fleshy protuberance (sometimes referred to as the gluteal fold), and between two imaginary lines, one on each side of the body (the "outside lines"), which outside lines are perpendicular to the ground and to the horizontal lines described above and which perpendicular outside lines pass through the outermost point(s) at which each nate meets the outer side of each leg . . .

—Part of a St. Augustine, Florida,
ordinance drafted by city commissioners to
regulate nudity on the beach and in restaurants

Yes, legalese can indeed give you a pain in the ass.

"literally," too much: Most of us know this, but for some reason, it's still a problem: The word "literally" is used too often and wrongly. Literally means ACTUALLY. It is not correct to use it to emphasize something. Repeat this three times. If "literally" is used wrongly, all sorts of strange things can start happening in prose. Wretchedly. And literally.

> Smith struck a match and relighted his pipe. He began to pace the room again. His eyes were literally on fire.
> —Sax Rohmer,
> *The Mystery of Dr. Fu-Manchu* (1913)

◇

> And with his eyes he literally scoured the corners of the cell.
> —Vladimir Nabakov, *Invitation to a Beheading* (1959)

◇

> Man, when I first met Christy—and this is no joke, a cliché but no joke—it was like my heart was literally stuck on my esophagus.
> —Ethan Hawke, *The Hottest State* (2006)

◇

> There was a tense silence, then a hard voice literally spat into the room: "Yes!"
> —A. E. van Vogt, *Masters of Time* (1950)

◇

The land literally flowed with milk and honey.
—Louisa May Alcott, *Little Women* (1868–69)

◇

Hopkins tied Tarver in knots from the opening bell—
literally and figuratively.
—AP news story about a boxing match (2006)

◇

His eyes ran, literally, across the whole of the upper
portion of his face . . .
—Richard Marsh, *The Beetle* (1897)

◇◇◇◇◇

literary and historical allusions, bad use of: Allusions to
great literature and the past make for more vivid, interesting writing. But in the hands of a wretched writer, things can get ridiculous:

As I prepare this script, tapping away at the keyboard
as Socrates might have done if he had owned a PC . . .
—Eammon McCabe,
BBC News Magazine (December 5, 2008)

◇

It was the best of times, it was the worst of times . . .
Little did Charles Dickens know when he penned the

opening lines of his classic Tale of Two Cities 149 years ago that it was a sentiment that could be applied to the U.S. album market last week.

—Alan Jones,
"Not Such Great Expectations
for the U.S. Album Market,"
Music Week (December 19, 2008)

◇

Sometimes too hot the eye of heaven shines, and often is his gold complexion dimm'd; and every fair from fair sometime declines. Shakespeare was not thinking about the shipping industry when he penned those lines, but shopping today has reason to reflect on the more prosaic truth behind the words . . .

—Moore, Stephens & Co. Chartered Accountants,
the bulletin "The Bottom Line"

◇

It was Gandhi who said, "there are people in the world so hungry, that God cannot appear to them except in the form of bread." That is unlikely to apply to Robert Schofield, boss of the UK's biggest food manufacturer, Premier Foods.

—Alex Beckett,
"Premier Hopes to Calm City Nerves
with Hovis Relaunch,"
The Grocer (September 6, 2008)

◇

Three thousand years ago Solomon said: "There is nothing new under the sun"; but if he could come back to this world and engage board at Eseeola Inn, he would find that something new has been invented; for he could hollow "halloo" in a telephone and receive an answer from a social-minded fellow in the telephone office over at Cranberry, and he could chalk his cue and try his luck on a billiard-ball, like which no rotary object ever revolutionized across a rectangular game-table in the city of Jerusalem.

—Shepherd M. Dugger,
*The Balsam Groves of the
Grandfather Mountain* (1892)

◇◇◇◇◇

luridness, bad: Some writers get positively peppy when it comes to grim, gory, unsettling, and otherwise unpleasant topics. Needless to say, this can be unnerving to the unsuspecting reader. He or she is merrily reading along when he or she is confronted with a detailed description of . . . well, say, pieces of people (which seems to be quite popular).

As Buck hung up, the door of the pub was blown into the room and a blinding flash and deafening crash sent patrons screaming to the floor. As people crept to the door to see what happened, Buck stared in horror at the frame and melted tires of what had been Alan's Scotland Yard-issue sedan. Windows had been blown out all up and down the street and a siren was already sounding. A leg and part of a torso lay on the sidewalk—the remains of Alan Tompkins.

—Tim LaHaye and Jerry B. Jenkins,
Left Behind (1995)

◇

Yesterday a young boy was run over in that street, where he was playing. Last year a speeding vehicle hit a little girl crossing the street, tearing her body apart. They gathered up her limbs in her mother's dress. Another child was kidnapped by professional criminals. After a few days, they released her in front of her home, after they had stolen one of her kidneys! Another boy was put into a cardboard box by the neighbourhood boys in a game, but was run over accidentally by a car.

—Muammar Qaddafi,
Escape to Hell and Other Stories (1998)

◇

The shot went through Freeman's head like a soft watermelon, raining pieces of him onto the screaming crowd.

—Dean Devlin and Roland Emmerich,
StarGate: A Novel (1994)

In a hellish blur, Bruno Torenzi whipped his arm around, plunging the scalpel deep into the puffy fold above Marcozza's left eye. With a good butcher's precision and hard speed, he cut clockwise around the orbital socket. Three, six, nine, midnight . . . The blade moved so fast, the blood didn't have time to bleed.

"ARRGH!" was a pretty good approximation of the sound Marcozza made.

He screamed in agony as the entire restaurant turned. *Now* everyone noticed Bruno Torenzi. He was the one carving the eye out of that fat man's face—like a pumpkin!

—James Patterson and Howard Roughan,
Don't Blink (2010)

Lest you think this is a relatively modern tendency, we introduce you to a group of older writers with an abiding penchant for the lurid. These poets from the early 1900s formed what we call "The Tabloid School of Poetry"—poetry that focuses on the rather ghastly with rather gleeful verve.

The case of Hardy Atwood I briefly will relate,
Though words fail to describe it or William Tyler's
fate.
They found poor William Tyler, his crushed and
bruised remains.

Wedged in among the fragments, wide scattered
  were his brains.

—Alexander B. Beard,
"The Great Boiler Explosion! at Hodges" (1888)

◇

Beneath me here in stinking clumps
Lies Lawyer Largebones, all in lumps;
A rotten mass of clockholed clay,
Which grown more honeycombed each day.
See how the rats have scratched his face?
Now so unlike the human race;
I very much regret I can't
Assist them in their eager "bent."

—Amanda McKittrick Ros, "The Lawyer" (1912)

◇

Oh, Heaven! it was a frightful and pitiful sight to see
Seven bodies charred of the Jarvis' family;
And Mrs Jarvis was found with her child, and both
  carbonized,
And as the searchers gazed thereon they were
  surprised.
And these were lying beside the fragments of
  the bed,
And in a chair the tenth victim was sitting dead;
Oh, Horrible! Oh, Horrible! what a sight
  to behold,

The charred and burnt bodies of young and old.
—William McGonagall, "Calamity in London" (1898)

And what better way to describe beautiful Westminster Abbey than this poem by Amanda McKittrick Ros:

Holy Moses! Take a look!
Flesh decayed in every nook!
Some rare bits of brain lie here,
Mortal loads of beef and beer.
—Amanda McKittrick Ros, "On Visiting
Westminster Abbey" (1933)

macho, too mucho (see also hipster writing, embarrassingly unhip, page 101): The wretched macho character appreciates women, and knows how to treat 'em right. Of course the babes all go for him. The discerning reader, however, does not.

The classic wretchedly macho man needs no introduction: He says what one expects.

"How do you like *my* version of the Dance of the Nile, Ruff?" she whispered in my ear.

"More!" I said.

Dames! Out here with seventy people using you for a pushball, they'll do anything! But get 'em in a closed room!

—Jimmy Shannon, *The Devil's Passkey* (1952)

But modern wretched macho writing goes to new levels. Bill O'Reilly, a master of wretched macho in his *Those Who Trespass*, offers us a tough guy character who causes women to "have multiple orgasms over a period of several hours." One only wishes for more, more, more, baby, more! (We are being facetious.)

> "Say baby, put down that pipe and get my pipe up."
> Stripping off her bathing-suit, she walked into the huge shower. She pulled the lime green curtain across the entrance and then set the water for a tepid 75-degrees. The spray felt great against her skin as she ducked her head underneath the nozzle. Closing her eyes she concentrated on the tingling sensation of water flowing against her body. Suddenly another sensation entered. Ashley felt two large hands wrap themselves around her breasts and hot breath on the back of her neck. She opened her eyes wide and giggled, "I thought you drowned out there, snorkel man."
> Tommy O'Malley was naked and at attention. "Drowning is not an option," he said, "unless of course you beg me to perform unnatural acts—right here in this shower."
> —Bill O'Reilly, *Those Who Trespass* (1998)

Macho writer Glenn Beck also knows his babes:

> Something about this woman defied a traditional chick-at-a-glance inventory. Without a doubt all

the goodies were in all the right places, but no mere scale of one to 10 was going to do the job this time.
—Glenn Beck, *The Overton Window* (2010)

Then there are the macho characters whose view of women is slightly, shall we say, *offensive*? (As in malodorous.)

I'm not much on the sex stuff, nor the lithe slenderness and gracefulness of women. Still, there was a suppleness to her body that made her seem to creep in and out of my arms without actually ever doing it. Get what I mean? The best way I can describe it is, that she clung to me like a wet sock.
—Carroll John Daly, *The Tag Murders* (1952)

Speaking of odd views of women:

Like most women, she got lubricated even while looking at nature shows of animals copulating, even though consciously the thought of being aroused by animals was repellent.
—David Brooks, *The Social Animal* (2011)

[Ed. note: Confession: One of us is a woman. She suggests that this is not the case.]

metaphors, confusing: Metaphors are a type of analogy (see analogies, bad and excessively extended, page 6) which make comparisons between two things that aren't alike but share some vital idea or characteristic that the writer wishes to make more vivid. "That guy is a shell of a man," uses "shell" metaphorically. You're not supposed to take the comparison literally; i.e., the competent reader doesn't think the guy is really a hollow shell. Unless the man has been eviscerated.

They are much like similes (see page 177), except similes use "like" or "as" in the phrase whereas metaphors do not; the comparison is implied. The key to writing good metaphors is to make comparisons that seem to make at least some vague sort of sense.

Some writers seem to miss this vital point.

> You got further plucking the chicken in front of you than trying to start on one up a tree. Especially when the tree was in another country, and there might not even be another chicken.
> —Robert Jordan, *The Path of Daggers* (1998)

◇

> When beholding the tranquil beauty and brilliancy of the ocean's skin, one forgets the tiger heart that pants beneath it; and would not willingly remember, that this velvet paw but conceals a remorseless fang.
> —Herman Melville, *Moby-Dick* (1851)

[Ed. note: Herman, Herman, Herman—a panting heart under the ocean's skin with a toothy paw? This is classic?]

Sometimes a metaphor is not so much confusing as tiresome. Tom Friedman's "steam" metaphor instantly steams into our own mental train station:

> And real conservatives would understand that the Tea Party has become the Tea Kettle Party. It is people in real distress about our predicament letting off steam by trying to indiscriminately cut everywhere. But steam without an engine—without a strategic plan for American greatness based on spending cuts, tax reform and investments in tomorrow—will take us nowhere.
> —Thomas Friedman, "Are We Going to Roll Up Our Sleeves or Limp On?"
> *The New York Times* (September 9, 2011)

metaphors, mixed: A mixed metaphor is a thing of beauty and a lead balloon hovering on the horizon. And we mean it. Yes, as you may have cleverly deduced, that was a mixed metaphor itself. And, yes, as you may also have cleverly deduced, mixed metaphors— wherein a nice, clean metaphor gets roughly grafted to another unrelated metaphor—run rampant in wretched writing.

Herewith a few examples:

I'm writing this story, first, because while researchers in a wide variety of fields have shone their flashlights into different parts of the cave of the unconscious, much of their work is done in academic silos.

—David Brooks, *The Social Animal* (2011)

◇

The argument was a peripatetic orang-utan, bouncing off the walls of their separate frustrations like a ping-pong ball in a wind tunnel.

—David Gerrold, *Chess with a Dragon* (1987)

◇

The baby boomers have dropped the ball on their burden of responsibility.

—Meghan McCain,
"Welcome to the Obamaclypse,"
The Daily Beast (August 10, 2011)

◇◇◇◇◇

modifiers, misplaced: Modifiers—whether they are words, phrases, or clauses—modify other words in a sentence. They are supposed to be helpful words or phrases that make a picture clearer for a reader. But some modifiers are not helpful. They shove their annoying heads in exactly the wrong place, in the wrong part of the sentence, modifying a word or phrase the writer didn't intend. The result: some very peculiar images.

Art mogul Charles Saatchi considers the works consumed in the East London Momart warehouse fire irreplaceable in the history of British art. "Hell," 2000, a 28-square-foot installation with hundreds of toy Nazis, by Jake and Dinos Chapman, is one of many pieces that set the art world aflame. Now a glob of burnt plastic, Saatchi reportedly spent $900,000 for the piece.

—Matthew Rose, "From Art to Ashes,"
Art & Antiques (Summer 2004)

[Ed. note: Contrary to this luridly constructed sentence, Mr. Saatchi is not a glob of burnt plastic. As far as we know.]

She was the kind who grew up with suitors, had powerful men with roses on their knees before her.

—Fay Weldon, "Inside the Whale" (1999)

[Ed. note: Granted, men could have tattoos of roses on their knees.]

After years of being lost under a pile of dust, Walter P. Stanley, III, left, found all the old records of the Bangor Lions Club.

—*Bangor Daily News* (January 20, 1978)

[Ed. note: While we supposed this technically could have been true, we have a hunch that Walter P. wasn't lost under dust, piled or otherwise.]

There was a whole family of planets . . . and I picked
out one that I named Beth, after my girl. She was
about five thousand miles in diameter . . .
                        —Clive Trent (Victor Rousseau Emanuel),
                              "Human Pyramid," *Spicy-Adventure
                                        Stories* (April 1941)

*[Ed. note: Apparently the protagonist likes his gals big and
healthy.]*

She wore a dress the same color as her eyes her father brought her from San Francisco.
                                  —Danielle Steel, *Star* (1990)

*[Ed. note: We have not (thankfully) read the novel, but we
presume her father brought her a dress, not her eyes, from
San Francisco, although both are possible, particularly in this
marvelous scientific age.]*

Elsas and other researchers say they believe that as-
partame can do more damage over a long period of
time than federal health officials.
                        —*The Lehigh Valley (PA) Morning Call*
                                        (November 4, 1987)

*[Ed. note: We are unwilling to go on the record as to the
damage-making abilities of federal health officials.]*

And, yes, I favor the death penalty for murderers of children, law-enforcement officers and all members of our community.

> —Then-political candidate Bernadette Castro,
> in a letter to the editor,
> *The New York Times Magazine*
> (September 4, 1994)

[Ed. note: Ms. Castro lost the election. Suggesting the death penalty for voters is not a great way to "win over the voters."]

He put the melting honey-colored fruit on her plate and got out a silk handkerchief. She began to eat it thoughtfully.

> —F. C. Phillips,
> "Romance for the Chambermaid" (c. 1885)

[Ed. note: Handkerchiefs, even when silk, are usually not very yummy.]

◇◇◇◇◇

non sequiturs: "Non sequitur" means "It does not follow" in Latin. In wretched writing, it means "It *really* does not follow." While in the hands of a skilled writer, a non sequitur can be a deliberate, humorous noncomment on a preceding statement; in the hands of a wretched writer, it is a huh?-evoking comment . . . leaving the reader flummoxed indeed.

If your mother had six fingers on one hand, you cannot distinguish between violet and black.

—Harry Stephen Keeler, *The Trap* (1956)

◇

"For a farmer, you seem very interested in the opposite sex."

—Terence Haile, *Space Train* (1962)

◇◇◇◇◇

obviousness, excessive: It seems that some writers feel a need to spell out the most obvious, most self-evident concepts to their readers. To wit:

The sun rose promptly at dawn.

—Tom Clancy, *The Teeth of the Tiger* (2003)

◇

Brilliant. Thank you, Mr. Clancy. We call this blatant tendency to state the obvious "the Duh! factor." Often it's a statement of logical obviousness.

He was sitting on a chair which happened to be near him.

—John Brunner, *The Shockwave Rider* (1975)

◇

The patron licked his fingers with saliva.
—Peter Thomas Senese and Robert Geis,
Cloning Christ (2003)

◇

"Sook, this is Dixon Mayhew," Jason said. "And this
is Dixie Mayhew, his twin sister." Dixie wore her hair,
the same color as her brother's, almost as short as
Dixon's, but she had dark, almost black, eyes. The
twins were certainly not identical.
—Charlaine Harris, *Dead as a Doornail* (2006)

*[Ed. note: Considering that one is male and one female, yeah,
they're not identical—good conclusion.]*

Other times, it's a matter of the most ridiculous rudimentary
reasoning:

Summing up, all child abuse is evil, and most abusers
are bad people.
—Bill O'Reilly,
A Bold Fresh Piece of Humanity (2008)

◇

Catholics as a rule avoid divorce—unless one of
them dies.
—Frank Corsaro, *Kunma* (2003)

Worst of all is the Duh! factor moment that is instead supposed to be a marvel of deductive skills.

> As she peered up at him, Jupiter suddenly realized she was a Gypsy. Her first words confirmed this. "I am Zelda, the Gypsy," she said.
>
> —Robert Arthur,
> *The Mystery of the Talking Skull* (1969)

> What was the meaning of all that apparatus? Racks of test tubes, most of them half-full; the microscopes on stands; the Bunsen burners; the white-painted box, on which was the word Incubator—what were these things? In a flash of intuition, Creighton realized the truth. He was in a laboratory.
>
> —James Corbett, *The Somerville Case* (1949)

And we, too, realize the truth. Duh.

◇◇◇◇◇

opening lines, appalling: The opening line of a book should "hook" the reader and, carrying our piscine metaphor further, enable the writer "to reel him or her in" and *read the entire book.*

Here are some bad fishermen-writers who used very, very dull hooks. Or to reverse the metaphor, these openers (or "hooks") make us want to "throw back the fish"—i.e., the book. And here we see the problems of confusing and dull opening lines with this, our very own opening "hook" for the "fish" which is this section. But read on . . .

> Have you ever visited that portion of Erin's plot that offers its sympathetic soil for the minute survey and scrutinous examination of those in political power, whose decision has wisely been the means before now of converting the stern and prejudiced, and reaching the hand of slight aid to share its strength in augmenting its agricultural richness?
> —Amanda McKittrick Ros, *Delina Delaney* (1898)

[Ed. note: McKittrick Ros is equally bad when it comes to opening poems, as the first line of her "Eastertide" demonstrates: "Dear Lord the day of eggs is here."]

> The void leered. Implacable hostility flattened itself against the frosty dark, awaiting the time to strike. Shocking danger fled away from him into the sucking emptiness, and cunningly eluded him, and ruthlessly returned. Timeless peril watched forever, with the cruel, cold eyes of the stars.
>
> Nicol Jenkins, spatial engineer, fought back silently.
> —Jack Williamson, *Seetee Shock* (1968)

◇

> The shriek detonated throughout the big house. It seemed to gather momentum rather than follow the laws of harmonics. The young gardener looked up

from the hedge he was clipping, mumbled something in an aside, then calmly returned to his task, a cheeky expletive on his lips. Farah, the maid in the kitchen looked up, raised her eyebrows and continued to scrape the grapefruit into the Minton dish. Nellie ran upstairs as soon as she heard the sound, she was the only one to act positively in the household, she knew her mistress was awake.

—Lorenzo Montesini, *Cardboard Cantata* (1986)

◇

A new voice hailed me of an old friend when, first returned from the Peninsula, I paced again in that long street of Damascus which is called Straight; and suddenly taking me wondering by the hand "Tell me (said he), since thou art here again in the peace and assurance of Ullah, and whilst we walk, as in the former years, toward the new blossoming . . .

—Charles M. Doughty,
Travels in Arabia Deserta (1888)

[Ed. note: Interestingly, the Arabians by most accounts hated this travel writer, finding him an insufferable bore.]

The silver light of the storm shifted perceptibly as though a black velvet curtain had fallen over the mountains, enclosing the girl in the small car into a cube of impersonal aloneness without destination. The morning's May sunshine, which had turned the sea to azured splendor, might have been a dream or one of those glazed picture postcards which traveling friends and relatives send from Cannes or Venice or, for that matter, Santa Barbara in California.

—Ruth McCarthy Sears,
Wind in the Cypress (1974)

Or while we're at it, Akron in Ohio . . .

◇◇◇◇◇

overwrought writing: It is laudable to be excited when writing about certain topics and, indeed, to convey that enthusiasm or passion to one's readers. But sometimes a writer gets a little overexcited, to put it mildly.

She is a swan of beauty and grace which sails through the portals of the mind into greater sunsets. She is an eagle that soars through the sky . . . Miss Eccles' mouth is a Grand Canyon of excellent speech . . . Moreover, her voice is a shark which swims from its mother's belly into the blue ocean. It is the bird which is tossed from the nest, and it flies. The play flew because of the skills of Julie Eccles, and the fact that she is glorious does not hurt!

—Review in *Capitol Currents*
(a newsletter published in Sacramento, California)
(September 1995)

And yet these selfish and ignorant meddlers—patriots, they have the gall to call themselves—they would stand in the path of destiny. What do they think they've accomplished? The lives of how many were saved tonight? Thirty thousand? Five times that many people die around the globe every day. They die in obscurity at the end of an aimless existence, and they disappear to dust as though they'd never been. But those thirty thousand, they would have died for a cause greater than any other, their names would have been etched in monuments in the new world, on the granite markers heralding mankind's new beginning. One world ruled by the wise and the fittest and the strong, with no naïve illusions of equality or the squandered promises of freedom for all. "How many times must we learn the same lessons? Leave the useless eaters to their pursuit of happiness, and the result is always slaughter and chaos and poverty and despair."

—Glenn Beck, *The Overton Window* (2010)

◇◇◇◇◇

overwrought writing about minor things: There's another type of overwrought writing that is equally wretched: We speak of that produced by writers who have the unique ability to turn on the emotional faucets and wax poetic about something most of us wouldn't really think twice about. These are the kind of people who figuratively grab the reader and (also figuratively) go on and on and on, fulminating passionately, not about global warming or something it is perhaps normal to be a little bit or a great bit passionate about, but about things that seem, well, kind of unimportant and not quite worth the breath (or paper). Minor things like . . .

The Padded Bra!

> And do they wear that lubricating lie,
> That fleshless falsehood! Palpitating maids
> Puff themselves out with hollow buxomness,
> To lead some breathless gaby at their heels
> A scentless paper chase!
> —Alfred Austin, *Fortunatus the Pessimist* (1892)

The Banana!

> Have you ever taken the time to stop and really contemplate one? It is heart-lightening to behold. As cheerful as a daffodil, but somehow more human. In

a bunch they look like fingers. Individually, they have skin as smooth as human skin and a gently curving shape that is perfectly evolved to fit the human grip. They are even satisfying to peel, unlike the mean and fiddly orange. There is the snap of the stem, then, as a silk dressing gown might fall with a whisper from the shoulders of a beautiful woman, it stands before you in all its pale, naked glory.

—Nigel Farndale,
"The Banana: Why Is It Such
an Object of Ridicule?"
The Telegraph (January 9, 2010)

The Pillow!

I only realized how important pillows were to my life when I checked into a room at the Carlyle and found that my pillowcases had been monogrammed—a small thing, but enough to evoke an emotional response: it was, to borrow a phrase from Daisy Buchanan, so beautiful it almost made me cry. It made me think about pillows seriously . . .

—Nick Foulkes, *The Carlyle* (2007)

The Actor John Travolta!

Tarantino's question remains, and remains unanswered. What did Travolta do? . . . In the firmament,

the brightest stars have the shortest lived: blue giant
to black hole. But the universe isn't old enough to en-
compass the degeneration which Travolta managed.
It will take 20 billion years for our sun to reach its ultimate state, frozen in crystalline indetectability. Travolta did it in 10.

—"Travolta's Second Act,"
interview with Martin Amis, *The New Yorker*
(February 20–27, 1995)

◇◇◇◇◇

participial phrases, dangling (see also modifiers, misplaced, page 130): A participle is a verb (usually ending in "-ing"
or "-ed") that does extra duty as an adjective or adverb. Together
with some other words, it becomes a participial phrase that modifies the meaning of a *specific* noun in a sentence. "Running down
the street, the boy shouted at the misbehaving dog." "Running
down the street" is a participial phrase. It modifies, or refers to,
"boy." Maybe this is not the most interesting of phrases, but it is
correct. This is not the case with our examples below.

These are participles doing something they shouldn't be doing. They're misbehaving—by dangling at the wrong end of the
sentence, modifying the wrong nouns. With ludicrous results.

Bad participles! Bad, bad participles!

The bouncer was watching him, black hair dripping
and shivering in the morning chill.

—A. A. Baker, *A Noose for the Marshal* (1990)

◇

A mountain lion suspected of killing at least two sub-urban dogs was shot to death after a state warden spotted it taking a report near the scene of the latest attack.

—Associated Press, 1995

◇

Grilled in foil or alongside a ham, turkey, or chicken, those who shied away from onions before will delight in their new found vegetable.

—Waldbaum's Foodmart circular

◇

On a late winter evening in 1983, while driving through fog along the Maine coast, recollections of old campfires began to drift into the March mist, and I thought of the Abnaki Indians of the Algonquin tribe who dwelt near Bangor a thousand years ago.

—Norman Mailer, *Harlot's Ghost* (1991)

[Ed. note: See? Even two-time Pulitzer Prize winners can blow it.]

Mereu stayed with 50 of Angius' 400 sheep, dressed in dirty and ragged canvas clothing and shoes with holes.

—Associated Press (December 18, 1987)

◇

Retired after 27 years as a domestic-violence coun-
selor with the Chicago police, the 71-year-old Mr. J.
went to college on a football scholarship, made an
All-America team, and briefly played in the NFL before joining an all-black league.

—The University of Chicago Magazine
(February 1996)

◇◇◇◇◇

penises, strange (see also breasts, strange, page 26): Just as
wretched writers strive to avoid the obvious when writing about
breasts, they do the same when faced with the male organ. Thus
penises are not the dull, ordinary snake or tube. Instead they
are . . .

Penis as Cashew (Changing to Fruit Then Veg)

He felt his cashew become a banana, and then a
rippled yam, bursting with weight.

—John Updike, *Brazil* (1994)

Penis as Pickle (Sweet)

The rosy, perky gherkin revealed before her eyes did
not frighten her . . .
—Isabel Allende, *Daughter of Fortune* (2006)

Penis as Poop (Piled)

[She] took his old battering ram into her lips. Uncle
was now as soft as a coil of excrement.
—Norman Mailer, *The Castle in the Forest* (2006)

poetic subject matter, dubious: When choosing a topic for
a poem, most writers aim for the sublime, the significant, or at
the very least, the nonridiculous. Wretched writers, however, opt
for the more minor, perhaps excessively *unique*, let us say, subject
matter. Or should we say stupid subject matter?

One master wretched poet and skilled dubious subject matter
picker was Samuel Wesley (1662–1735), who wrote about topics
such as rotting ducks (*On a Supper of a Stinking Duck*), just plain
maggots (*On a Maggot*), a chatty chamber pot (*A Dialogue Between Chamber-Pot and Frying Pan*), that always scintillating
poetic trope—body and/or head lice (*A Pindarique on Three
Skipps of a Louse*)—and mellifluously grunting hogs (*A Pindarique
on the Grunting of a Hog*).

Harmonious Hog draw near!
No bloody Butchers here,
Thou need'st not fear,
Harmonious Hog draw near, and from thy beaute-
    ous Snowt . . .
Harmonious Hog! warble some Anthem out!

Others have risen—or descended—to Wesley's level. Matthew Green (1697–1737) and his "The Spleen" immediately springs to mind:

I always choose the plainest food
To mend vicidity of blood.
Hail! water gruel, healing power,
Of easy access to the poor . . .
To thee I fly, by thee dilute—
Through veins my blood doth quier shoot;
And by swift current throws off clean
Prolific particles of spleen.

Poet/dentist Solyman Brown's (1790–1876) masterwork "The Dentologia: A Poem on the Diseases of the Teeth" focuses on the sadly underpoeticized topic of tooth decay:

Whene'er along the ivory disks, are seen,
The filthy footsteps of the dark gangrene;
When caries come, with stealthy pace to throw
Corrosive ink spots on those banks of snow—
Brook no delay, ye trembling suffering fair,
But fly for refuge to the dentist's care.

And Lillian Curtis (fl. 1870s) offers us a romantic paen to "The Potato" (i.e., the tuber):

> The useful and the beautiful
> Are not far apart we know.
> And thus the beautiful are glad to have,
> The homely looking Potato.

Speaking of teeth and potatoes, two final selections . . .

From *My Last Tooth* (by an unknown American poet, 1890s):

> Farewell, old tooth . . .
> That tainted my breath,
> And tasted as smells
> A woodpecker's nest.

And this classic of potato bug extermination poetry, aptly named "Potato Bug Exterminators," by James McIntryre:

> Now for a minute, lend your luggs,
> our theme it is potato bugs.

[Ed. note: James McIntryre (1827–1906) usually wrote about large cheeses, earning him the moniker Poet Laureate of Cheese, but we feel his underappreciated Potato Bug poem deserves special attention.]

politicians and pundits turned novelists, pathetic sex scenes and: Let us briefly address a very specific subset of wretched writers. We speak of politicians and political pundits who decide that they are novelists and manage to get their novels published by large, well-known publishers.

> *[Ed. note: We are not convinced the fact of being accepted and published is due to the literary quality of said works. Or are we being cynical?]*
> *[Ed. note: Nah.]*

Most often these Washington insiders write, as you might expect, political thrillers based on their Washington inside knowledge. All well and good. But when one looks at excerpts for their work—particularly their ostensibly racy sex scenes, one deduces that while they might have knowledge about politicians and the inner workings of Washington, they do not seem to have much knowledge of good writing. Or for that matter, good sex. Take these six—examples. (Please take them. We don't want them anymore and you will see why.)

> Suddenly the pouting sex kitten gave way to Diana the Huntress. She rolled onto him and somehow was sitting athwart his chest, her knees pinning his shoulders. "Tell me, or I will make you do terrible things," she hissed.

Even though it had been only minutes since their last lovemaking, John Mayhew was as ever overwhelmed by the sight of her, the shameless pleasure she took in her own body and its effect on him. Since he wasn't sure what to say, he made a production out of lighting up and enjoying that first, luxurious afterbout inhalation.

—Former Speaker of the
House Newt Gingrich, *1945* (1995)

◇

Okay, Shannon Michaels, off with those pants!

Ashley was now wearing only brief white panties. She had signaled her desire by removing her shirt and skirt, and by leaning back on the couch. She closed her eyes, concentrating on nothing but Shannon's tongue and lips. He gently teased her by licking the areas around her most sensitive erogenous zone. Then he slipped her panties down her legs and, within seconds, his tongue was inside her, moving rapidly . . .

—Television host Bill O'Reilly,
Those Who Trespass
(1998)

◇

She romped on top of Simolzak's huge frame, straddling him with her hands on his chest, her back arched and her breasts flailing wildly in the air. Her back was to him and her long hair swung from side to side as if accentuating the abandonment of her screams.

—Senator Jim Webb (D-VA), *Lost Soldiers* (2002)

◇

I set the edge of my teeth halfway up her breast, just at the point of tension but not, so far as I could tell, of pain. This was the sweetest flesh I had ever tasted, including fish and fowl.

—Former Governor of
Massachusetts William Weld,
Stillwater: A Novel (2002)

◇

He could feel her heart beneath his hands. He moved his hands slowly lower still and she arched her back to help him and her lower leg came against his. He held her breasts in his hands. Oddly, he thought, the lower one might be larger.

—Former vice-presidential aide
I. Lewis (Scooter) Libby, *The Apprentice* (1996)

◇

As he drew nearer and removed her T-shirt and panties, she began to moan deeply and loudly. Loudly and deeply. In the midst of their heat, such a state of abandon was reached that the normally voyeuristic Jack, who liked to watch himself make love, actually fell from the bed onto the hot radiator. But, like the Indian fakirs who can be on a bed of nails without later showing puncture marks, Jack did not scorch or burn, nothing visible remaining except a small soreness days later.

Once he was inside her, she began to cry and shudder in a series of small convulsions. He had never been with a woman who reacted like this and was both surprised and excited by her abandon.

Her cries became veritable screams as she moaned, and her eyes became glassy with passion. As Jack continued to bring Sara to an increasingly greater state of tension and release, tension—a violent begging for release and then the convulsive wave—her screaming became threatening.

—Radio host Michael Savage,
Abuse of Power (2012)

pretension, pseudo-philosophical prose and: The pseudo-philosophical writer seems to think that philosophy, instead of meaning "love of wisdom" means "love of saying stuff that doesn't necessarily make sense but is pompous and sounds kind of cool." And sadly, there are different ways of doing this in wretched writing.

On one hand, we have the pseudo-philosopher writing something that means absolutely nothing. He or she will toss in cryptic sentences and "daring" concepts, so that it (theoretically) sounds intelligent, mystical, Zen-like, or all of the above. Of course, it (actually) sounds ridiculous.

> [T]he Hussein Chalayan vessel I wore at the Grammys wasn't inspired by a chicken. It was stolen from an egg. But the transformation, the context, and the approach taken to reinterpret the meaning of birth and rebirth in terms of fame on a fucking red carpet—this is what creates the modernity of the statement. The past under-goes mitosis, becoming the originality of the future.
>
> —Lady Gaga,
> "From the Desk of Lady Gaga:
> Memorandum No. 1,"
> *V Magazine* (May 1, 2011)

◇

> We're all toenails on our own bodies . . . Time is flesh and flesh is gravity. Gravity is time and time is velocity.
>
> —Uri Geller, *Shawn* (1990)

On the other hand—and this is more common with columnists—we have the pseudo-philosopher ascribing extremely heavy and truly ridiculous meaning to the pedestrian. (To be nonphilosophical, we call this "throwing shit into the game" or simply "bullshitting.)

> It is perhaps the closest thing to a collective orgasm. That instant when the ball hits the back of the net and the nation is united in a paroxysm of mutual euphoria . . .

Perhaps this is what the Epicureans had in mind when they talked of the moral supremacy of hedonism . . .

—Matthew Syed,
"Latent Euphoria of Future as Yet Unwritten,"
The Times of London (June 2, 2010)

◇

Certainly, chairs that are expensive, yet useless, one-offs are testimonies to our crisis of nihilistic self-loathing, but, as a narrative means, four legs and a seat have a limited expressive range.

—Stephen Bayley,
"This Chair Has Still Got Legs,"
The Observer (August 22, 2009)

◇◇◇◇◇

prose, preposterously Proustian: Marcel Proust, considered by many to be the father of the modern novel, wrote a very long book (over 1.5 million words) that, to many of us who are not literature professors, is also a very boring book. Nevertheless critics say it is one of the greatest books ever written. One of Proust's goals in his very long book was to elucidate the passage of time via describing *all* the little things that happen to us in everyday life. Whether or not this worked for Proust (there is some debate) is not the point; what *is* the point is that it certainly does not work for some other writers. We think you will agree as you (try to) read these long passages on toothbrushing, toe wiggling, and television watching, respectively.

[S]he squeezed a little water into a plastic container and put a few dabs of toothpaste on her brush. She slipped the brush into her mouth and pressed the small button in the end which activated its electric motor. The bristles—soft, gentle bristles, guaranteed not to damage the enamel or the gum—moved swiftly against the teeth. She began with the top left molars, worked round to the bicuspids, and came round again from them to the incisors, the canines, the laterals and the centrals. Once she had reached the front of her mouth, she changed her grip on the brush so that it moved round to the top right, travelling over the bicuspids and molars as it moved. Coming down the sides of her teeth, she paused and took a deep breath, placed a little more paste on the brush and moved round again this time beginning with the actual chewing surface of [the] upper right molars, coming round and cleaning again between the crevices until she had worked round to the left-hand molars.

Once more she put paste on the brush in this same elaborate ritual and concentrated her attention now on the inside of the upper left molars . . .

—John E. Muller (Lionel Fanthorpe),
Dark Continuum (1964)

◇

Joshua wiggled his toes. The four smaller ones had really very little to say. To be sure, there was a symmetry in the arc they formed that was rendered with subtlety and taste, like a quartet of doughty pillars steeped and graded for harmony of thought and action. Reassuring in its way but at a sacrifice, a sense of restraint; the subjugation of the individual for the common good: conformity. All in all, good architecture but not great art.

On the other hand, there was the big toe. THE BIG TOE. No humble petitioner, a craggy tower—intense, feverish, excessive. Not only above but beyond the crowd. Proud, insolent, a testimony to personal commitment. The nail—jagged, splintered, uncompromising; a pioneer. A tuft of hair-like fire in the desert—stark, defiant, liberated. The superstructure itself, a thousand planes and textures, the face of the people, and yet, free-forming, spontaneous, beauty through truth, the soul of the artist bared.

—Walter Koenig,
Buck Alice and the Actor-Robot (1988)

◇

After using the washroom, he wandered into the lounge and sat down. The inviting decor, padded leather booths and lively music created a relaxing atmosphere. Pressing his BlackBerry handheld to his ear, he listened to his messages. Making a mental note to return the calls later, Warrick slid the phone into his pocket and stared up at one of the flatscreen TVs.

He checked the score of the Mariners game, relieved to see his team was beating the Yankees. An

American Airlines commercial came on and he thought of Tangela. He wondered if she was out with her friends. On the weekend, she liked to go with her coworkers to the Karaoke Hut for cocktails. Singing off-key and encouraging others to do the same was something he couldn't get behind, but Tangela always seemed to enjoy herself.

—Pamela Yaye, *Love on the Rocks* (2010)

◇◇◇◇◇

prose, purple: Purple prose—the art of writing prose so ornate, so flowery, and so overweighted with frills that the reader not only gets exhausted but also feels as though he or she is being smothered in highly scented velvet curtains—is a time-honored hallmark of wretched writing.

We must give a special nod to Edward Bulwer-Lytton. His work has spawned the annual Bulwer-Lytton awards, given to the person who can write the worst first sentence of an ersatz novel. Herewith the first sentence of his *real* novel:

It was a dark and stormy night; the rain fell in torrents—except at occasional intervals, when it was checked by a violent gust of wind which swept up the streets (for it is in London that our scene lies), rattling along the housetops, and fiercely agitating the scanty flame of the lamps that struggled against the darkness.

—Edward Bulwer-Lytton, *Paul Clifford* (1830)

While Bulwer-Lytton is (justly) famed for his "dark and stormy night" line, there are other writers who deserve attention for their peculiar penchant for the purple. Here we have a landscape as if seen from above. A very, very, very, very well-adjectived landscape.

> Syria and Greece, Italy and Spain, laid like pieces of a golden pavement into the sea-blue, chased, as we stoop nearer to them, with bossy beaten work of mountain chains, and glowing softly with terraced gardens, and flowers heavy with frankincense, mixed among masses of laurel, and orange, and plumy palm, that abate with their grey-green shadows the burning of the marble rocks, and of the ledges of porphyry sloping under lucent sand. Then let us pass farther towards the north, until we see the orient colours change, gradually into a vast belt of rainy green, where the pastures of Switzerland, and poplar valleys of France, and dark forests of the Danube and Carpathians stretch from the mouths of the Loire to those of the Volga, seen through clefts in grey swirls of rain-cloud and flaky veils of the mist of the brooks, spreading low along the pasture lands.
>
> —John Ruskin,
> *The Stones of Venice*, Volume 2 (1853)

And the purveyors of purple prose keep purveying it—even now in the twenty-first century.

> Edward in the sunlight was shocking. I couldn't get used to it, though I'd been staring at him all afternoon.

His skin, white despite the faint flush from yesterday's hunting trip, literally sparkled, like thousands of tiny diamonds were embedded in the surface. He lay perfectly still in the grass, his shirt open over his sculpted, incandescent chest, his scintillating arms bare. His glistening, pale lavender lids were shut, though of course he didn't sleep. A perfect statue, carved in some unknown stone, smooth like marble, glittering like crystal.

—Stephanie Meyer, *Twilight* (2005)

[Ed. note: All right already. He shines. He shines. He shines. We get it.]

Rapid sonorous beats of turmoil and uncertainty pulsed in his head to near unimaginable proportions as the potential ramifications perpending if what he expected to discover was to come true overtook him.

—Peter Thomas Senese and Robert Geis,
Cloning Christ (2003)

◇

The branch Roran had added to the fire burst asunder with a muted pop as the coals underneath heated the gnarled length of wood to the point where a small cache of water or sap that had somehow evaded the rays of the sun for untold decades exploded into steam.

—Christopher Paolini, *Brisingr* (2008)

◇◇◇◇◇

punctuation, too cleverly avoiding: Punctuation is the use of those little marks—such as periods, commas, colons, apostrophes, and dashes—that make sentences easier to read and understand. Some wretched writers prefer not to use them maybe because they think it makes their writing sound more spontaneous more like real talking or something or maybe because it makes it them sound more intellectual or enigmatic like the great writers William Faulkner or James Joyce who didnt use punctuation at all in the last chapter of Ulysses but we think this all outside of great writing makes it all a bit wretched as in this piece written by Bob Dylan who is a great musician but in terms of writing is no James Joyce.

> aretha/crystal jukebox queen of hymn & him diffused
> in drunk transfusion wound would heed sweet sound-
> wave crippled & cry salute to oh great particular el
> dorado reel & ye battered personal god but she can-
> not she the leader of whom when ye follow, she can-
> not she has no back she cannot . . .
> —Bob Dylan, *Tarantula* (1972)

[Ed. note: The astute reader may note that Dylan didn't like capital letters either; but did like the ampersand (&) instead of "and." The book opened to many bad reviews but has recently been rereviewed by some intrepid souls more positively as an example of great surrealistic writing. On the other hand, another recent reviewer said, "The originality is eventually overcome by stupidity." This seems fair.]

Writer James Frey sometimes shows bad punctatory behavior as well, but in a less ambitious manner (as may be expected).

> He said she would have a better life the sun shining every day more free time less stress she said she would feel like she had wasted a decade trying to get to the major leagues only to demote herself once she got into them.
>
> —James Frey,
> *Los Angeles, Bright Shiny Morning* (2008)

◇◇◇◇◇

redundancy, regular: Redundancy is unnecessary duplication. It is not necessarily a bad thing. In engineering, for example, it may be a good thing to have an extra cable for your suspension bridge, in case one snaps during a windstorm or earthquake. But deadly perils such as falling off a bridge rarely affect prose. Why then, you may ask, do so many writers use an extra figurative "cable" in the "bridge of writing" (to belabor a metaphor)?

We do not know. We merely know that there are great numbers of extra "cables" out there . . .

> Aro started to laugh. "Ha, ha, ha," he chuckled.
> —Stephanie Meyer, *Twilight* (2005)

◇

> "Dr. Martin, my name is Holmes, Bradley Holmes," said Holmes by way of introducing himself.
> —Frederick Eberhard, *The Skeleton Talks* (1933)

◇

Her bare feet, though grimy, were caked with dirt.
—Elizabeth Sinclair, *Gardens of the Moon* (2009)

◇

The pain she felt was palpable.
—Kathi Appelt, *The Underneath* (2008)

◇

She made him feel as a man should feel. Essentially male.
—Emma Darcy, *His Boardroom Mistress* (2004)

◇

The annular rings turned.
—Gregory Benford, *In the Ocean of Night* (1977)

◇

This was very significant and important.
—Charlaine Harris, *Club Dead* (2003)

◇◇◇◇◇

redundancy, repetitive: What do you get when you take simple redundancy and square it? Why, repetitive redundancy, of course! In this type of wretched writing, it is not enough to simply repeat a point. One must repeat the exact *word(s)* as well. Thus one doubles the obviousness and doubles the stultifying prose. It is enough to sicken the reader and make him or her sick.

> She sneered at him, her beautiful mouth twisted into an ugly sneer.
> —Robert Sheckley, *The Laertian Gamble*
> (Star Trek Deep Space Nine, No. 12) (1995)

> Little ridges of muscle ridged his jaw.
> —Brad Ward, *The Spell of the Desert* (1951)

> To understand why the house makes so much money at the craps table, you first have to understand why.
> —Roger Gros,
> *How to Win at Casino Gambling* (1996)

> Of all the things to think, he never thought he'd think that . . . Eubanks looked annoyed. He exhaled annoyingly and said . . .
> —Aaron Rayburn, *The Shadow God* (2005)

repetition (or epizeuxis), excessively repetitive: The wretched writer often follows the dictum: If it sounds good once, why not repeat it five or six times? And then do it again. Yes, when overdone, the literary device epizeuxis—the repetitive use of phrases or words for effect—can be, in a (repeated) word, annoying, annoying, annoying.

Our favorite notable enthusiast of this sort of wretched writing is a writer who has appeared many times before in this collection, but who deserves a special shout-out for his trademark epizeuxitic skills. We speak of course, of sci-fi writer Lionel Fanthorpe, who wrote under varied pseudonyms, turned out over 180 books, 89 of them in a three-year period while he was also holding down a teaching job, and under each of those names and in all of his books had a remarkable tendency toward repetition. Following are some of the best examples, examples, examples:

> They had chosen their time very well indeed! The city slept. Men slept. Women slept. Children slept. Dogs and cats slept.
>
> —Leo Brett (Lionel Fanthorpe),
> *March of the Robots* (1961)

◇

> Everywhere was dark, dark darkness. Blackness. Black. Black blackness.
>
> —John E. Muller (Lionel Fanthorpe),
> *A 1,000 Years On* (1961)

Mr. Fanthorpe is not alone in his excessive epizeuxisty, if we may coin the term. Exuberant repetition is also found frequently in academia, as in the following passage from NYU professor

D. G. Leahy. In this case the reader is assaulted by equivocal predication. Univocally.

> *Total presence breaks on the univocal predication of the exterior absolute the absolute existent* (of that of which it is not possible to univocally predicate an outside, while the equivocal predication of the outside of the absolute exterior is possible of that of which the reality so predicated is not the reality . . . the identity of which is not outside the absolute identity of the outside, which is to say that the equivocal predication of identity is possible of the self-identity which is not identity.
>
> —D. G. Leahy,
> *Foundation: Matter the Body Itself* (1996)

◇◇◇◇◇

rhetorical questions, terrible: A rhetorical question is a question that is not intended to be answered. Often a rhetorical question is what is termed *aporia*—the narrator asks questions of him or herself. ("Where should I begin?") Sometimes it is *anacoenosis*—the writer is asking the opinion of his or her audience. Other times it is termed *epiplexis*—asked to rebuke or reproach. ("Have you no shame?") But there is another type of rhetorical question that we are most interested in exploring: the *rhotten* rhetorical question.

Sometimes a rhetorical question is rhotten because it simply sounds ridiculous, even insane:

> Indeed, what had his aunt's unhappy demise from a super-power ray to do with tortoise-shell spectacles?
> —Harry Stephen Keeler,
> *The Mysterious Mr. I* (1938)

◇

> There are some sounds in nature which are anathema to man. For most people they are confined to the strangled screaming of a vixen in heat, hideous and unearthly in the black voids of a sleepless night. The question you have to ask yourself here is, "Am I most people?"
> —Bernard King, *The Destroying Angel* (1987)

[Ed. note: The question we are asking ourselves is: Why am I reading this?]

This afflicts academics as well . . .

> The most important consequence might well be that the theory of autopoetic systems seems to bar all ways back to an anthropological conception of man. It precludes, in other words, humanism . . . This means we have to invent new conceptual artificialities in order to give an account of what we see when we

meet someone who looks and behaves like a human being. How do we know that he is one?

—Niklas Luhman,
"The Individuality of the Individual,"
Reconstructing Individualism (1986)

[Ed. note: Our follow-up rhetorical question: "Will you ever shut up, Mr. Luhman?"]

So why do writers ask such terrible rhetorical questions? That, of course, is in and of itself a rhetorical question.

◇◇◇◇◇

rhymes, facile: Ever notice how "dog" rhymes with "bog" rhymes with "log"? Of course you did. And we did, too. But certain versifiers appear to be enthusiastically swept up by what appears to the rest of us to be extremely simple rhymes. In fact, they are so swept up that they use said simple rhymes to express rather simple concepts.

The result is facile poetry at its best (or rather, worst). For example, we have poet/actor Charlie Sheen:

When the clock's final ticking exposes your day
It's your balls we'll be clipping in the dock of
    your bay

—Charlie Sheen, "The Big White Phone,"
A Peace of My Mind (1990)

Nineteenth-century poet Fred Emerson Brooks utilizes a daring eagle/beagle rhyme:

> Fear not, grand eagle
> The bay of the beagle!
> —Fred Emerson Brooks, "Old Eagle" (c. 1890s)

And here we have a complex sigh/eye theme:

> I loved the gentle girl,
>   But oh! I heaved a sigh,
> When first she told me she could see
>   Out of only one eye.
> —Lillian Curtis, "Only One Eye" (fl. 1870s)

◇◇◇◇◇

rhymes, painful: The wretched writer who prefers to express him or herself in rhyme often chooses a creative way to surmount one particular obstacle: the obstacle of not having a proper rhyming word in mind to convey a thought. Rather than give up the thought, said wretched rhyming poet instead opts to push an almost-rhyme in there, much like squeezing a foot into too small a shoe. The result is equally painful.

> Gooing babies, helpless pygmies,
> Who shall solve Fate's engimas?
> —J. W. Scholl,
> "The Light-Bearer of Liberty" (1899)

◇

Sad, on Broadway next afternoon,
I strolled in listless manner,
Humming her most detested tune,
And smoking an Havana.
　　　—Francis Saltus Saltus, "In a Book-Store" (1890)

◇

I remember it well, as she was smilin'
She said it was called Turtle Island.
　　　　　　　　　　　　　—Britney Spears,
　　　　　　"Honeymoon Poem" (November 8, 2004)

◇◇◇◇◇

romance, unromantic: A love scene can be a thing of beauty and a joy forever. But in the wrong hands, something goes wrong. Horribly wrong.

Unromantic "Love at First Sight" Moment

Her feet were tiny and topped off with pale nail polish. Not seeing any visible corns or bunions, Paulo mentally checked that off his list. An admitted foot man, her feet were definitely lickable.
　　　　　　—Koko Brown, *Player's Ultimatum* (2011)

Unromantic Kissing Scene That Stinks (Literally)

Erik plunged his hands into the soft tangle of her hair, pulling her head back gently, then sank into her mouth again. He tasted desire, heat, and a mild hint of tuna.

—Meg Benjamin, *Long Time Gone* (2010)

[Ed. note: In case you are wondering about the unromantic case of halitosis, the heroine had just eaten a tuna sandwich that the hero had ordered for her at a diner. Ergo, we assume this is supposed to be a little cute touch. But we find it fishy . . .]

Unromantic Kissing Scene That Sucks (Figuratively and Literally)

"Adams won't like this," she said, and turned with a smile which was for him alone to let him take her, and helped his heart find hers by fastening her mouth on his as though she were an octopus that had lost its arms to the propellers of a tug, and had only its mouth now with which, in a world of the hunted, to hang on to wrecked spars.

—Henry Green, *Concluding* (1948)

Unromantic Kissing Scene That Explores the Chemistry of Love (Literally)

As Julia and Rob semi-embraced, they silently took in each other's pheromones. Their cortisol levels dropped . . . Later in their relationship, Rob and Julia would taste each other's saliva and then collect genetic information.

—David Brooks, *The Social Animal* (2011)

[Ed. note: Q: What reader could fail to be transported by these lines? A: Any reader would fail to be transported. This was a trick question.]

◇◇◇◇◇

"said" synonyms: "Said" is the word most commonly used by writers to denote a particular action, that is, saying something. But many writers seem to feel that "said" is too pedestrian, too easy, too *nonwriterly*. Why use "said," these writers ask, when there are so many other fine words instead?

Why not indeed?

Well, for one thing, most writers believe in "show, don't tell." In other words, what is being said should be strong enough to stand on its own without added color commentary (in the form of a descriptive non-"said" verb) by the writer. For another, in not using "said," anti-said zealots often come up with bizarre contortions to avoid saying "said."

"He's done it," fanged out Rake.
—John Fonville, *Where the Big Gun Rides* (1961)

◇

"You goddamned right we got you," iced Wes.
—John Fonville, *Where the Big Gun Rides* (1961)

◇

"Got you spotted," he apostrophized the hidden rifleman.
—Leslie Scott, *The Brazos Firebrand* (1953)

◇

"What," I monosyllabled.
—Florence May Pettee,
"The Clue from the Tempest" (1921)

◇

"Opal . . ." she hoarsed.
—Michael Avallone,
The Case of the Violent Virgin (1957)

◇

"I was," he emanated darkly.
—Jacquelyn Frank, *Hunting Julian* (2010)

Some writers are repeat "non-saiders" to the nth degree. Novelist Desmond Wilcox, for example, seems to hate the word. In his *Future Tense* (1987), his characters almost never "say" or "said." In only three consecutive pages, they taunt, hyperbolize, tease (with aggravating reluctance, to boot!), vacillate, inveigh, vituperate, tantalize, sooth, expiate, provoke, affirm, chastise, and dehort.

Stephanie Meyer, author of the *Twilight* series, similarly is anti-said; in fact, she seems congenitally incapable of using "said" more than once on a page. Unfortunately she lacks the creativity of some of her "said"-hating predecessors. She shows instead an inordinate fondness for such bland "said" synonyms as "muttered" and "moaned." But what she lacks in creative quality, she more than makes up in quantity. A quick thumbing through of about fifty pages reveals the following plethora of "said" euphemisms: pointed out, challenged, called, teased, sighed, whispered, finished, muttered, groaned, protested, sighed, admitted, moaned, accused, promised, grumbled, verified, mumbled, fished, laughed, exhaled, bargained, and allowed.

This, of course, leaves the reader with one question: "Hey, Steph, don't your characters ever just *say* something?"

◇◇◇◇◇

saying nothing: A good writer uses words to communicate something—an idea, a viewpoint, an event, *something*. A wretched writer uses words to fill the page. The words make coherent sentences, yes, and may even sound as though something were being conveyed. But at the end, the reader is left thinking, "What?"

> Ultimately slippery slope arguments are a mixed bag.
> They are useful as a way to reinforce good dogma,

but they are also used to reinforce bad dogma. Similarly they can scare us away from bad policies and good policies alike. There are good slippery slope arguments and bad ones for good ends and bad ends.

—Jonah Goldberg, *The Tyranny of Clichés* (2012)

Okay, so slippery slope arguments can be useful for good things or useful for bad things. And good or bad in general about good and bad things. We don't know about you, but we feel a tad less than edified. But it sure sounded good! Or bad!

Alan Greenspan, the Federal Reserve chairman who successfully didn't predict the greatest housing recession in history since the 1930s, was a master of saying nothing as well. It used to be thought that this was deliberate, but some now wonder. The University of Virginia Writing Program Instructor Site collects the back-and-forthing of Greenspan to illustrate how not *not* to say anything. To wit:

Risk takers have been encouraged by a perceived increase in economic stability to reach out to more distant time horizons. But long periods of relative stability often engender unrealistic expectations of it[s] permanence and, at times, may lead to financial excess and economic stress.

—Alan Greenspan,
Federal Reserve Board's semiannual
Monetary Policy Report to the Congress,
The Committee on Financial Services,
U.S. House of Representatives, July 20, 2005

◇◇◇◇◇

sentences, lamentably long: It seems that some writers set a challenge for themselves: how to write the longest sentence possible. Some of these writers turn out very long, but very interesting long sentences. James Joyce comes to mind. But other writers are like people who talk too fast and forget to breathe and overwhelm you with a sea of verbiage.

These writers are no pikers. When they write a long sentence, they write a long sentence. They go on and on and on. And they don't stop. They're marathoners, no question. Herewith, some entries in the Lamentably Long Sentence Marathon:

Clocking in at 86 Words . . .

James nodded his thanks, opened the wax paper and looked a bit suspiciously at the offering, it looked to be a day or two old and suddenly he had a real longing for the faculty dining room on campus, always a good selection of Western and Asian food to choose from, darn good conversation to be found, and here he now sat with a disheveled captain who, with the added realization, due to the direction of the wind, was in serious need of a good shower.

—Newt Gingrich and William Forstchen,
*Pearl Harbor: A Novel of
December 8th* (2009)

And at 135 Words . . .

The Middle Ages, by which people mean the Christian Middle Ages, the European Middle Ages, had their faults, like any other epoch, but to call Islamofascism medieval is to equate medieval Christendom and the medieval Islamic world, a religion that gained adherents through persuasion and a religion spread almost entirely by the sword, a civilization that abolished slavery and a civilization that propagates it, a society that began poor and ended rich and a society that began rich and ended poor, a culture that was backward in the beginning and enlightened in the end and a culture that was enlightened in the beginning and backward in the end, a polity that was weak and divided and became strong and, well, divided, and a polity that was strong and relatively united and became weak and divided.

—Jonathan David Carson,
"Islam Is Not Medieval," *American Thinker* (2006)

And the Winner at 166 Words . . .

The precision of the absolutely minimum transcendence of the dark is the light itself/the absolutely unconditioned exteriority of existence for the first time/the absolutely facial identity of existence/the proportion of the new creation *sans* depth/the light itself *ex nihilo*: the dark itself univocally identified, i.e., not self-identity identity itself equivocally, not the dark itself equivocally, in "self-alienation," not "self-identity, itself in self-alienation" "released" in and by "otherness," and "actual other," "itself," not the abysmal inversion of the light, the reality of the darkness equivocally, absolute identity equivocally predicated of the self/selfhood equivocally predicated of the dark (the reality of this darkness the other-self-covering of identity which is the identification person-self).

—D. G. Leahy,
Foundation: Matter the Body Itself (1996)

◇◇◇◇◇

similes, bad: To use a simile—a literary device comparing two different things usually using the words "like" or "as"—a good simile is like a helpful friend. To use another simile, a bad simile is like, well, a . . . bladder of lard.

[Ed. note: Bladders of lard are generally not considered helpful friends.]

And speaking of bladders of lard . . .

He stood trembling like a bladder of lard . . .
—Bron Fane (Lionel Fanthorpe),
The Thing from Sheol (1963)

◇

Dan was the kind of man to whom panic and fear were as alien and foreign as green spotted pseudopods.

—Pel Torro (Lionel Fanthorpe),
Formula 29X (1963)

[Ed. note: In fairness to Fanthorpe, we must admit that green spotted pseudopods are indeed alien and foreign. That said, we hold that it is still a bad simile.]

While bad similes are often overwhelmingly present in bad novels, otherwise fine writers can also fall prey to the bad simile—often as a result of being excessively creative. (Or perhaps tired. We are not sure.) To wit:

I came suddenly, a jolt that emptied my head like a spoon scraping the inside of a soft-boiled egg.

—Jonathan Littell, *The Kindly Ones* (2009)

◇

[The rain] bloated the sky full like a fat goose, and when it fell, it was as if some celestial knife had slit the fat goose belly and splashed the innards onto the land in monstrous conflagration.

—Mike McQuay, *Pure Blood* (1985)

◇◇◇◇◇

technical description, excessive: One type of wretched writing that tends to be specific to the thriller genre (especially the techno-thriller) is an addiction to technological description. Preferably the kind of description that has numbers and brand names and other superspecific info in it. Writers who fall prey to this overwhelming overtechnical excess never use a basic noun when they can prove that they've read and mastered every technical manual about that noun on the planet.

A "gun", then, is never simply a "gun." It is:

> A Heckler & Koch MP-7, the successor to the old MP-5. The MP-7 was a short-barreled machine pistol, compact and powerful. In addition to the MP-7, Scho-field carried a Desert Eagle semi-automatic pistol, a K-Bar knife, and, in a holster on his back, an Armalite MH-12 Maghook, a magnetic hook that was fired from a double-gripped gun-like launcher.
> —Matthew Reilly, *Scarecrow* (2003)

◇

> "Those capabilities include," Zack explained, "four internal rotator fed ammunition clips which load a custom-modified lightweight short-barreled internal-recoil-compensated 5.56mm M249 machine gun . . ."
> —Matthew Reilly, *Scarecrow Returns* (2012)

Similarly, a jet is not your basic plain vanilla jet. And neither, of course, is a helicopter your basic plain vanilla helicopter. And neither, of course, is any flight on said jet or helicopter just a simple flight . . .

> He was sitting all alone in the enormous cabin of a Falcon 2000EX corporate jet as it bounced its way through turbulence. In the background, the dual Pratt & Whitney engines hummed evenly.
>
> —Dan Brown, *The Lost Symbol* (2009)

◇

> On Friday morning of the August week in 1990 when Iraq invaded Kuwait, Lieutenant General Chuck Horner was at 27,000 feet, cruising at .9 Mach (540 knots), and nearing the North Carolina coast. He was headed out to sea in the Lady Ashley, a recent-model Block 25 F-16C, tail number 216, that had been named after the daughter of his crew chief, Technical Sergeant José Santos. Horner's aide, Lieutenant Colonel Jim Hartinger, Jr., known as "Little Grr," was on Horner's left side, a mile out, slightly high. Horner and Hartinger were en route to a mock combat with a pair of F-15Cs out of the 1st Tactical Fighter Wing (TFW) at Langley Air Force Base in Tidewater Hampton, Virginia: a winner-take-all contest that would match wits and flying skills. After that, they were all scheduled to form up and return to Langley AFB as a flight of four aircraft.
>
> —Tom Clancy, *Every Man a Tiger* (1999)

technical writing, technically bad: Technical writing explains a technical topic in such a way that we English major types can understand it. Theoretically. But as you have probably guessed, this isn't the case when it comes to *bad* technical writing. Bad technical writing doesn't explain said tech topic; it instead irritates the reader. And it typically does so in one of four ways.

First, there's the very common "Repeat or Rephrase" method of bad technical writing. In this case, the technical writer avoids having to think too hard about how to explain something difficult and simply rearranges the words . . . or sometimes doesn't even bother rearranging them but simply repeats them. The result is accurate, of course. But somehow . . . unenlightening . . .

> The primary function of voltage sag mitigation is to mitigate and overcome voltage sags in the system.
> —From *The IET Power Engineer* magazine, Volume 2 (2008)

There's the Extremely Detailed, but Deadly Dull method . . . which typically causes the reader to stop reading.

> Over the years, the Department of Energy has received numerous inquiries . . . particularly from school-aged children, who were interested in understanding more about the Department's inventory of depleted uranium hexafluoride . . . The Department put together the following "fun facts" . . .

> DUF6 Cylinder Weight Comparisons A Ticonderoga-class cruiser is about equal in weight to 706 cylinders of depleted uranium hexafluoride (DUF6). It would take over 70 cruisers to weigh more than the Nation's inventory of DUF6! The Navy owns only 27 Ticonderoga-class cruisers.
>
> DUF6 Cylinder Weight Comparisons 7,142 cylinders of DUF6 weighs as much as a Nimitz-class aircraft carrier. The entire inventory of 57,634 cylinders weighs more than all eight of the Navy's Nimitz-class aircraft carriers combined!
>
> —From a U.S. Department of Energy website, the "Fun Facts for Kids" section

Similarly, there's the "Too Technical" method. Here the writer apparently gives up explaining and just goes ahead being supertechnical. The reader is thus superconfused.

> OILATUM CREAM is especially effective if applied immediately after washing, when the normal acid condition of the skin may be disturbed and when the sebum content of the stratum corneum may be depleted.
>
> —Label, Oliatum Cream, Stiefel Laboratories

And finally, the "Almost as Bad as a Bureaucrat" method—which speaks for itself. Or rather, doesn't.

> There appears to be some confusion over the new pilot role titles. This notice will hopefully clear up any misunderstandings . . . The Landing Pilot is the Non-Handling

Pilot until the decision altitude call, when the Handling Non-Landing Pilot hands the handling to the Non-Handling Landing Pilot, unless the latter calls "go-around," in which case the Handling Non-Landing Pilot continues handling and the Non-Handling Landing Pilot continues non-handling until the next call of "land" or "go-around," as appropriate.

—From a British Airways
operations manual for pilots

◇◇◇◇◇

thesaurus addiction: Some wretched writers take to the thesaurus like others take to the bottle. They pack their writing with long, polysyllabic words when a nice simple one-syllable word would do just as well. In fact, it'd do better. At least we'd understand what is being said—without having to resort to a dictionary, thesaurus, or comforting drink ourselves.

The wretched writer surely knows that the average reader won't know the meanings of these words, yet he or she uses them anyway. Here are three typically very annoying examples.

Lancinations of unendurable ecstasy ravened through his consciousness, starbursts of warring sensory impulses that slipped once more to coherent phenomena, an instant before his mind shattered to follow into final chaos.

—Karl Edward Wagner, "The Dark Muse" (1975)

◇

This is strictly a pantagraphic hauntography of proto-mantic motherworlds. Mysteriograms of toposonic radiances are deconstructed and raptoluminal reso-nances at residual numinophillic nemeta sites are reit-erated in the mycoboreal precincts . . .

—Press release publicizing the music
of the band Infernal Methods

And speaking of residual numinophillic nemeta sites, let us close with one final example. (Which, according to the book jacket, is the author's "most accessible book to date." This makes us very worried about his prior books . . .)

Indeed dialectical critical realism may be seen under the aspect of Foucauldian strategic reversal—of the unholy trinity of Parmenidean/Platonic/Aristotelean provenance; of the Cartesian-Lockean-Humean-Kantian paradigm, of foundationalisms (in practice, fideistic foundationalisms) and irrationalisms (in prac-tice, capricious exercises of the will-to-power or some other ideologically and/or psycho-somatically buried source) new and old alike; of the primordial failing of western philosophy, ontological monovalence, and its close ally, the epistemic fallacy with its ontic dual; of the analytic problematic laid down by Plato, which Hegel served only to replicate in his actualist monova-lent analytic reinstatement in transfigurative reconciling dialectical connection, while in his hubristic claims for absolute idealism he inaugurated the Comtean, Kierkegaardian and Nietzschean eclipses of reason, replicating the fundaments of positivism through its transmutation route to the superidealism of a Baudrillard.

—Roy Bhaskar,
Plato Etc.: The Problems of Philosophy and Their Resolution (1996)

Frankly, we couldn't have put it better or more fideistically ourselves.

◇◇◇◇◇

translations, bad: Translating a written passage from one language to another is difficult. The main difficulty is knowing both languages well enough. Certain intrepid wretched writers, blithely unconcerned with their linguistic prowess, seem to say boldly (paraphrasing a certain Admiral Farragut), "Damn the foreign vocabulary and grammar, full speed ahead!" The results are what you might expect: a linguistic shipwreck.

ACT ONE: Carmen, a cigarmakeress from a tobago factory loves Don Jose of the mounting guard. Carmen takes a flower from her corsets and lances it to Don Jose . . .

ACT TWO: The Tavern. Carmen sings. (Aria: "The sistrums tinkling.") Enter two smugglers ("Ho, we have in mind a business.") Enter Escamillio, a Balls fighter. Carmen refuses to penetrate because Don Jose has liberated her from prison. He just now arrives. (Aria: "Slop here who comes.") . . .

ACT FOUR: A Place in Seville. Procession of Ballfighters . . . (Aria and chorus: "Toreador. Oreador. All hail the Balls of a toreador.") Enter Don Jose (Aria: "I besmooch you.") Carmen repels him. She want to join with Escamillio now chaired by the crow. Don Jose stabbs her. (Aria: "Oh, rupture, rupture.") He sings: "Oh, my subductive Carmen."

> —Program for the Genoa Opera Company's
> production of *Carmen* (1981)

◇

Far up the river your journey is through mostly primary forest with impenetrable undergrowth, Giant Orchids, Mangrove flowers, hugetress with puthon crapping for branches, tropical bulfrongs . . .

> —In a travel brochure from a Kalimantan,
> Indonesia, travel agency

◇

Here, you shall be well fed up and agreeably drunk. In the close village you can buy jolly memorials for when you pass away.

> —In the brochure for an Italian hotel
> in the Dolomites area

◇

You are properly exhausted after journey or business work. Worthily divert yourself from boredom and create new sense of perception that makes you completely relaxed & happy, please call on LONGMAN HOTEL where our multifunctional recreations will surely feast your tastes. YOU ARE ADDED WITH FUN

Welcome to Piano lounge where you could enjoy abundant beverages besides cocktails in an elegant atmosphere while being introxicated With pianists famouse musics from home and aboard.

YOU ARE AN EXTRAORDINARY VOCALIST AT KAROKE

—In a brochure from the Longman Hotel,
Shanghai, China

There is also a subset of wretched writers who do seem to know the languages they are working with, but choose, with a similar exuberance to the unschooled translators, to render bizarre, obscure translations that make the original in the foreign tongue, in this case, Latin, seem easier than the (translated) English. In normal English, the first line is translated from the Latin as "Otho's head is very small." But read on . . .

Otho's scooped nut its pusillanimity,
Erius' rustic semen-looted cruor,
subtile, levitating petite fume who's Libo,

see, no? If this phenomena incurred your
bite and Fuficius' senile recoction.
—Catullus, *Gai Valeri Catulli Veronensis Liber*,
trans. Celia and Louis Zukofsky (1969)

◇◇◇◇◇

trying too hard to impress the reader: Writing to impress
others is the equivalent of an older bald man trying to impress
and pick up cute twenty-something girls by driving around in a
shiny new Porsche. It doesn't work. It shouldn't be done. It makes
the older Porsche owner look ridiculous. It's also very unaesthetic
in a world that needs more beauty.

Writers usually try to impress readers by showing off their
immense knowledge of obscure words since writers rarely make
enough to afford Porsches. This doesn't work either. And they can
even make it worse . . .

Here's one example in which the writer "cleverly" mixes obscure words with ostensibly hip words in talking about a politician
accused of being a pedophile for preying sexually on teenagers:

[He] may or may not be a predator, but pedophiles
don't dig post-pubescent teens; *ephebophiles* do.
—Jonah Goldberg,
Los Angeles Times (October 6, 2006)

*[Ed. note: Do we "dig" the juxtaposition between "dig" and
the technical word "ephebophile"? Do we think it's a vital*

point that sexual predation on those older than thirteen is technically not pedophilia, because "pedophilia" is derived from the Greek word for "child," whereas "ephebophile" refers to teenagers? Do we think that Goldberg should just give up and buy a Porsche instead? (No. No. Yes.)]

Critics are especially prone to the "let me impress you with my Porsche-like words." We assume this is because they get tired of simply saying something like "the music sounded great" or "I liked the show a lot." Instead we're presented with overstuffed sausages of sentences.

> Here Liam's reflective paean to perseverance oscillates soberly between a single titular mantra and bursts of keening melodica from Noel until both dissipate . . .
> —Rock critic Pete Paphides on an Oasis album,
> *The Times of London* (October 1, 2008)

◇

> In memory of Jacques Derrida, let us observe that "The Lost Prince" is a drama of spectation. Or, rather, it purports to be. In fact, this is a movie that emphasizes visual transactions and expresses anxiety . . . As a result, "The Lost Prince" stands as a bright critique of the ecstatic scopophilia for which "Masterpiece Theater" has always stood.
>
> —Virginia Heffernan,
> "A Royal Son, Both Unseeing and Unseen,"
> *The New York Times* (October 15, 2004)

[Ed. note: Ecstatic scopophilia = Good shows. Really good shows.]

But most modern would-be-impressive writers pale when compared to Sir Thomas Urquhart (1611–60), known by some as the world's worst writer. As one blown-away critic noted, he writes with "a pedantry which is gigantesque and almost incredible." We are sure you will agree (if you can manage to get through the following passage):

> Why, I could truly have enlarged my discourse with a choicer variety of phrase, and made it overflow the field of the readers understanding, with an inundation of greater eloquence and that one way, tropologetically, by metonymical, ironical, metaphorical, and synecdochical instruments of elocution, in all their several kinds, artificially effected, according to the nature of the subject, with emphatical expressions in things of greater concernment, with catachrestical in matters of meaner moment . . . I could have used, for the promptlier stirring up of passion, apostrophal and prosopopoeial diversions; and, for the appeasing and settling of them, some epanorthotic revocations and aposiopetic restraints . . .
>
> But I hold it now expedient, without further ado, to stop the current of my pen . . . and write with simplicity.
>
> —Sir Thomas Urquhart,
> *The Jewel (Ekskybalauron)* (1652)

[Ed. note: Some say Urquhart wrote this way deliberately, as a sort of joke against the reader. It seems to us to be a rather cruel joke to inflict upon innocents.]

◇◇◇◇◇

unfortunate turns of phrase: We speak here not of double entendres, per se (for a discussion of this, see double entendres, unintended, page 76), but of phrases that can be taken to mean something else nonsexual. Something vivid. Something evocative. Something that sounds pretty silly. Something we can only assume (and hope) that the writer did not intend. Some unfortunate examples:

> And they had a wonderful sail on the dancing trimaran all the way around Acadia Park Island and back to a great clam dinner. That night in bed afterwards Loolie brought it up again.
>
> —James Tiptree Jr.,
> "Forever to a Hudson Bay Blanket" (1972)

◇

> Before, however, the moon had glided more than a soundless pace or two on her night journey, Myfanwy and her incomparable ass were safely out of sight . . .
>
> —Walter de la Mare,
> "The Lovely Myfanwy" (1925)

*[Ed. note: While we are sure Myfanwy has one heckuva pos-
terior, we feel confident that Mr. de la Mare is not referring
to this, but rather to the animal underneath said posterior.]*

He wasn't going to leave Pat Benson on her own,
crabs or no crabs.
> —Guy N. Smith, *Night of the Crabs* (1989)

*[Ed. note: Personally, we'd stay away from Pat. Or at least
not let her sit on our living room sofas.]*

◇◇◇◇◇

verbing: Once again we address that common wretched writing
problem of excessive creativity. In this particular case, it is exhib-
ited in the construction of verbs from other parts of speech, the
"gifting," if you will (to use a new noun-based verb that has unfortunately shoved aside the old-fashioned "giving"), to us of new
and creative verbs. We call this "verbing." We also call it "bad."

The sun mid-morninged.
> —Dean W. Ballenger, *Gunslinger Justice* (1976)

◇

Madness seethed in him, and his mind bleared toward the mica glitter of mute mineral matter.
> —Adam Lee, *The Dark Shore* (1996)

◇

She bent down again, profaned against her back, and pulled.

—Keith McCarthy,
The Silent Sleep of the Dying (2004)

Some writers seem to say to themselves, why am I restricting myself to mono-verbing? Why don't I multi-verb?

Kirk clipped . . . Chekov bolted . . . He malaised . . . Kirk distilled.

—Diane Carey and Dr. James I. Kirkland,
Star Trek: First Frontier (1995)

Other times, the new verb has real potential for catching on, but not quite the way the author intended.

"What the hell is this all about?" Hara demanded.
"Damnit, I thought I made it clear that you weren't to do any private dicking."

—Milton K. Ozaki, *Maid for Murder* (1955)

[Ed. note: Is public dicking, however, allowed?]

◇◇◇◇◇

villains, bad: Villains are, by definition, supposed to be bad. But in the case of wretched writing, there are *bad* bad villains—in other words, villains that just don't quite work . . .

In this fantasy novel, we have a villainous evil chicken that is not a chicken.

> The bird let out a slow chicken cackle. It sounded like a chicken, but in her heart she knew it wasn't. In that instant, she completely understood the concept of a chicken that was not a chicken. This looked like a chicken, like most of the Mud People's chickens. But this was no chicken. This was evil manifest.
> —Terry Goodkind, *Soul of the Fire* (1999)

Goodkind tries, we'll grant him that, and the reader who is caught up in the novel probably won't mind this passage. But there is something distinctly unfrightening about said faux chicken.

Another rather unthreatening villain comes from a very confusing and tortuously written Western, *Border Town* (1967), by Tom Coburn. He is the oh-so-cleverly named "Ah Hell" (yes, he is Chinese) and works for a Chinese smuggling ring, headed by Quo Wong, the "half-caste" son of an English lord. Not only is his name ridiculous, but he speaks in such painful dialect that the reader isn't as much scared as aching to give the fellow some money to buy Rosetta Stone English lessons. To wit, "Ketchem bossy-man Herb? Heap good. Too much Quo Wong Mexican hop. Blekfas leady now."

But the honor of the most ridiculous villain ever conceived goes to the creation of one of the worst writers ever, Harry Stephen Keeler. In his *X. Jones of Scotland Yard* (1936), the police posit about the "Flying Strangler-Baby," a killer midget who disguises himself as a baby and stalks victims by helicopter. (Keeler is also responsible for one of the worst names for a villain, the inappropriately monikered Kinkella MacCorquodale, who is, as one might guess from the name, a dreaded Mafia boss. Of course.)

◇◇◇◇◇

word creation, public relations and advertising: Public relations, advertising, and marketing writers deserve special credit for a special type of bad writing. We speak of the creation of incredibly contrived words that (theoretically) help promote a product or service. (These words typically have a shelf life of about four press releases . . . and for good reason.)

There are several ways PR writers and their ilk bring forth their creations:

The "Add a Suffix" System

> Full colour images and a *zoomify* feature allows you
> a close up look . . .
>
> —From the EziBuy catalog

[Ed. note: Yes, the old word "zoom" would have worked just as well. But it wouldn't have sounded as modern.]

Train + Ing
Traing

—Advertising slogan for
East Japan Railway Company
(which is posted throughout Japanese train stations)

[Ed. note: Yes, it is not "training," and no, we don't get it either.]

The "Add a Suffix and a New Meaning" System

Is your on-boarding process fragmented? Have you lost control of employee on-boarding? Are you manually sending and receiving information from IT, Finance and other departments? Are you simply using a time-consuming, error prone, manual employee on-boarding process? Using Nintex technologies, Antares can automate the most complex employee on-boarding processes. Ensure new hires get everything they need for their first day while taking the burden out of on-boarding for HR. Integrate communication between departments, organisation-wide, to drastically improve the speed and reliability of the on-boarding process. First impressions for new hires are everything, starting with employee on-boarding.

—Advertisement for Antares Solutions,
an IT consulting firm

[Ed. note: On-boarding is making new hires comfortable in their new positions. Or as we've always called it, "welcoming them."]
[Ed. note: Or as we now call it, "on-welcoming them."]

The "Mash Two Words Together to Get a Bad New Word" System

The creative vision for the campaign was driven by the growing demand from travelers for socially designed spaces and amenities. The "Meet You There" tagline acts as an invitation to experience key brand elements through clever headlines and energetic images of people gathering in different settings. "Wi-Fi, Mai-Tai, Say Hi" shows guests coming together, seamlessly blending business and leisure—also known as "bleisure."

—Press release,
"Sheraton Hotels Launches New $20 Million
Advertising Campaign on the Heels of
Successful Multi-Billion Rebranding Effort"
(June 21, 2011)

The "Mash Three Words Together" System

We are one of the only companies that can provide full mocial benefits to our customers!
—In a press release received by tech writer
Dan Rowinski, ReadWriteWeb

[Ed. note: The three words are "mobile," "local," and "social."
And yes, many people think it's just mobile plus social leading
some tech people to complain that the "local" is missing.
Frankly, we think the whole thing stinks.]

◇◇◇◇◇

words, wrong: We speak here not of often misused words
such as "penultimate" (often used to mean "ultimate" instead of
"next to ultimate") or "bemused" (in place of "amused"). No, the
wretched writer has a knack for creatively choosing *different*
wrong words.

Sometimes the misused words are quite basic—words such as
"illegible," "emancipate," etc.

> He rolled onto his back, and an illegible cry tightened
> the muscles in his thick neck.
> —Della Van Hise, *Killing Time* (1985)

[Ed. note: We rarely—if ever—have thought of cries and
their ability or inability to be easily read.]

> The lamp's glow was very weak compared to the blue
> glow emancipating from the basement.
> —Aaron Rayburn, *The Shadow God* (2005)

[Ed. note: Unless the author meant to say the blue glow was
freeing the basement. But then, how do you emancipate
from?]

Yes, Mr. Rayburn's *The Shadow God* is uniquely emancipated, so to speak, from correct usage of numerous basic words.

It infiltrated his lungs, filling them with a kind of innovativeness he had never felt before.

> Spiers's eyes popped extraneously from their sockets, as his face turned from a deep red to a sickly purple.
>
> —Aaron Rayburn,
> *The Shadow God* (2005)

Sometimes the wrong word problem arises when a writer wants to sound erudite and/or poetic and chooses words that sound erudite and/or poetic—but sadly, the *wrong* ones.

> They were featureless and telic, like lambent gangrene.
>
> —Stephen R. Donaldson,
> *White Gold Wielder* (1987)

True, "lambent gangrene" sounds very cool. But we don't usually think of gangrene as glowing. As for "telic"? It means "tending toward an end." So . . . um, huh?

Perhaps the ultimate basic word definition problem comes from Stephanie Meyer, the writer of the bestseller *Twilight*, who apparently has not grasped the technical nuances of the word "none."

> None of them, especially [Mr. Sparkle], glanced my way anymore.
>
> —Stephanie Meyer, *Twilight* (2008)

All of these wrong words make us so frustrated we want to rush off a cliff to our deaths in the Arctic Ocean. You know, like those rodents—lemurs.

> The abbot watched dazedly as they rushed like lemurs towards destruction.
>
> —Frank Corsaro, *Kunma* (2003)

◇◇◇◇◇

zoological sexual encounters, politician-writers and:

For some reason, a surprising number of politicians, political aides, and politically oriented pundits turned (bad) novelists incorporate animal sex in their works. We are not sure why. In fact, we are not sure if we want to know why. We merely point this out and submit several passages of wretched zoological sex scenes for your edification.

A Writer and a Bear

> Even an animal respects a man's desire, if it wants to copulate with him. Doesn't a female bear try to please a herdsman when she drags him into the mountains as it happens in the North of Iraq? She drags him into her den, so that he, obeying her desire, would copulate with her? Doesn't she bring him nuts, gathering them from the trees or picking them from the bushes? Doesn't she climb into the houses of farmers in order to steal

some cheese, nuts and even raisins so that she can feed the man and awake in him the desire to have her?
—Former Iraqi president Saddam Hussein,
Zabiba and the King (2000)

Another Writer and Another Bear

At age ten the madam put the child in a cage with a bear trained to couple with young girls so the girls would be frigid and not fall in love with their patrons. They fed her through the bars and aroused the bear with a stick when it seemed to lose interest . . . Is there feeling?" a bucktoothed man asked. "At least on the first night, after a bear?"
—Former vice-presidential aide
I. Lewis (Scooter) Libby, *The Apprentice* (1996)

The Same Writer and a Deer

At length he walked around to the deer's head and, reaching into his pants, struggled for a moment and then pulled out his penis. He began to piss in the snow just in front of the deer's nostrils . . . He asked if they should fuck the deer.
—Former vice-presidential aide
I. Lewis (Scooter) Libby, *The Apprentice* (1996)

[Ed. note: The answer is yes, they should.]

A Writer and Two Horses

[Ed. note: Here, the politician in question takes a less hands-on approach. In other words, she writes of animals having sex together, and removes the human component (except as watchers).]

A ton of finely tuned muscle, hide glistening, the crest of his mane risen in full sexual display, and his neck curved in an exaggerated arch that reminded Greg of a horse he'd seen in an old tapestry in some castle in Europe Jane had dragged him to. The stallion approached, nostrils flared, hooves lifting with delicate precision, the wranglers hanging on grimly . . . The stallion rubbed his nose against the mare's neck and nuzzled her withers. She promptly bit him on the shoulder and, when he attempted to mount, instantly became a plunging devil of teeth and hooves . . . Greg clutched the rails with white knuckles, wondering, as these two fierce animals were coerced into the majestic coupling by at least six people, how foals ever got born in the wild.

—Senator Barbara Boxer,
A Time to Run (2005)

The Writer and a Chicken

Imagine a man who buys a chicken from the grocery store, manages to bring himself to orgasm by penetrating it, then cooks and eats the chicken.

—Political pundit David Brooks,
The Social Animal (2011)

[Ed. note: No, we prefer not to imagine this, thanks.]

EPILOGUE

One of our favorite wretched writers, Harry Stephen Keeler, ended a mystery of his with a sealed page at the end, so you couldn't peek and find out whodunit. It's easier for our readers, who already know who did it when it comes to wretched writing: anyone and everyone who has ever written a line or more of prose or poesy, including, we must confess, ourselves. Just for the record, while doing this book, we found two—among many—examples of wretched writing from our own works: one of them the abysmal poem "Man Smell," the other a truly incomprehensible sentence in a nonfiction work that was happily edited out by an astute editor. We mention this to reiterate the important truth that every writer at any time can commit the crime of writing wretchedly, blithely unaware that this is happening. (This, of course, is why God created editors . . .)

Let us also reiterate that determining whether writing is wretched is, to a large degree, subjective. Something we consider wretched may be considered great reading material by others. But, of course, there are also those examples that scale the heights (or plumb the depths, more aptly) of wretched writing—and with these, there is little dispute as to its wretchedness. Whether it's one of the repeat offenders or a writer who happened to have a

bad day, a wretched writer's output is something to be appreci-
ated, to be savored, to be learned from, and to be celebrated. And
maybe to serve as a cautionary admonition the next time one feels
compelled to sit at the computer and vomit forth "deathless"
prose or poetry.

In closing, as a supreme caution, we offer the final stanza of
what has been called the worst poem ever written in the English
language, "A Tragedy" (and it is) by Théophile Marzials.

> I can dare, I can dare!
> And let myself all run away with my head
> And stop
> Drop.
> Dead.
> Plop, flop.

Plop.

INDEX